FINDING SPIRITUAL PEACE

Through Understanding
God's Work
In Your Life

LEX ADAMS

Spirit of Truth Publications
P.O. Box 2979
Minden, NV 89423

FINDING SPIRITUAL PEACE

Published by Spirit of Truth Publications
P.O. Box 2979
Minden, NV 89423

International Standard Book Number 0-9643206-2-2
All Scripture references are from
the King James version of the Bible

*Dedicated to my loving, wise,
and supportive wife, Lynn.*

CONTENTS

INTRODUCTION

The biblical promise of blessing and joy to God's people is repeated throughout Scripture. God speaks of complete joy, abundance in blessings, healing, deliverance, protection, comfort, peace, and every other possible good thing one could ever desire. And He speaks of it in terms of experiencing it today, not only when we get to heaven. Our difficulty is learning how to receive His blessings, and to listen to His voice of instruction and guidance. We easily miss the path because of a lack of understanding, which if we had it, would cause us to be overtaken by His blessings and goodness. The secret is not in seeking the blessings, but in learning to yield the inner self-will to God, and allowing God to accomplish His inner work of transformation in our hearts.

Life is often difficult. As Christians, we can become discouraged, confused, and bound by the many things which touch our lives, which for a time we may not understand. These very things are often the doors through which God would bring us into His life of blessing. God's most abundant blessings are for those who learn to think as Jesus would, in every situation of life, not merely those things such as church, worship, and Christian service. This book is written to help the believer make sense out of the many different "testings" we endure, and allow God to use them to bring us into His purposes, blessing, and peace.

Scripture is rich with words of encouragement, examples of the struggles and victories of others, and God's insight into everything that may touch our lives. However, seeing the answers is not always easy. It is our fervent prayer that these writings may help you find a greater peace, a deeper joy, and a fresh comfort in the circumstances in which you find yourself. This is possible as we seek to learn what the Holy Spirit is trying to teach us in each situation. God's goal is for us to mature into the likeness of Jesus, to have inner peace and joy, and to glorify His name. Our challenge is to learn how to cooperate with the Holy Spirit, to seek to be teachable, and to yield our *hindering* self-life to Him. As we learn these lessons, we also are granted the privilege of receiving and enjoying some of our inheritance here, today! May the Holy Spirit minister, as only He can, to the needs of your heart through the teachings in this book.

1

FINDING INNER PEACE
AND JOY

Heavenly Father, we come to seek a greater ability and strength to quickly obey the promptings of Your Spirit in our lives. Make us sensitive to Your touch and the whisper of Your guidance. Cause us to yield our self will to Thee and learn to exercise the power of our will to choose Your ways, as You make them clear to our hearts. Oh, Father, it is only in obedience that we find joy and clarity of understanding. Give us strength to obey in the face of our weakness. In Jesus' name we pray. Amen.

"ON EARTH PEACE, GOOD WILL TOWARD MEN."
(Luke 2:14)

At the birth of Jesus, shepherds in the field were visited by an angel and overshadowed by the glory of God. The angel told them of the birth of Jesus, the Savior, Christ the Lord. Then suddenly there was a whole host of angels praising God and saying, "glory to God in the highest, and on earth peace, good will toward men" (Luke 2:13-14). One angel came to give the message of "good tidings of great joy, which shall be to all people", but the excitement of the message was such that a great number of other angels burst upon the scene praising God. This was history changing news being given to these shepherds. The spiritual beings of heaven understood the magnitude of what was taking place. This was the *main event* for all of history. There was overflowing excitement in heaven over Jesus' coming and His purpose.

Often we may find ourselves saying, "well, that's just wonderful that the angels are all excited, but I'm down here struggling through life and I don't feel all that excited or blessed about anything. That is a nice message, peace and good will and all, but I don't feel it. I don't have this peace. I don't feel excited about my faith and my walk with Jesus." The angels said it was a message of great joy! We may feel like, "great, but where is it? It somehow got lost between the manger and me in my life." Why does the joy escape us? Why is peace elusive all too often?

One thing is sure, peace and joy are here, and they are for every believer in Jesus. We know this because it is promised in the Bible. That being the case, we can then seek understanding about how to find this peace and joy and live a life full of them. Problems and challenges touch each of us. They are real, and they hurt and stretch us. We feel the pressure of many different circumstances and we watch as it seems one after the other presses against our lives. Jesus told us, in John 15:11, "These things have I spoken unto you, that my joy might remain in you, and that your joy might be full." The Lord's joy came from His inner desire and delight in doing the will of the Father. Psalm 40:8 reads of Jesus, "I delight to do thy will, O my God." This is part of the key to walking in peace and joy, learning to delight in doing God's will. We should not seek to do works to please God, but inwardly in the heart and mind learn to obey God. Works follow!

What things did Jesus say to us so that His joy would be in us, and our own joy full? In the first 10 verses of the fifteenth chapter of John, Jesus gives several clear instructions to finding joy. Abide in Him, and allow Him to abide in us. This sounds simple enough, but how does it work? It means choosing, when we are pressured to respond to a matter wrongly and in self will, to listen to His inner voice and obey Him, not yielding to the voices of the flesh and the devil. Stay put in the Spirit is what he tells us. Don't fall into the lower nature response of wrong for wrong. If we are hurt, forgive, do not speak evil in return. If we are taken from, forgive, do not take back. If we are mistreated wrongfully and unfairly, suffer it, do not seek to get even. These are not easy responses to deliver. Our nature fights such yielding. However, it is in learning to react like Jesus did that we will open the doors of peace and joy, although the doors may seem very heavy to push open at times. I Peter 2:19-23 sets forth the example of Christ in suffering and responding in a manner pleasing to God. It also tells us that we are called to the same response. We are called to respond in all things as Jesus did. This is not possible, unless we are yielding to the Holy Spirit and the light of God's Word in our moments of testing. As odd as it may seem, the challenges and pressures that come are brought so we may learn to enter into the joy of the Lord. The doors on the palace of joy and peace are titled by many names which seem strange to our natural mind. One door reads, "Suffering wrongfully and not reacting." Another reads, "Being spoken evil of when it is not true, and loving and forgiving the person who said it." Yet another reads, "Pray for those who despitefully use you." And another states, "Do good to them that hate you." And one reads, "Love ye your enemies" (Matt. 5:44; Luke 6:27-36). Why? So that bitterness and resentment cannot get a root hold on our hearts and cut us off from the joy of God. We do not need to pray that people continue to mistreat us, but we can pray that God would become real in the lives of those who appear at the moment to be our "enemy." After all, Jesus died for them too! That in itself is a thought we would like to avoid when we are smarting from the mistreatment of another. But, Jesus loved them, forgave them, prayed "Father forgive them for they know not what they do," and we are called to do the same.

Jesus also tells us to obey His commandments. To do this we must be filled with the Word of God and obey what we learn. If we hold anything more precious than pleasing God, we will find testing coming in that area. Our possessions, our employment, our family, our wants and dreams, our self-efforts, must one by one be brought into subjection to God before we can find peace and joy. If we hold onto them, placing more importance on maintaining them than on obeying the Lord, we forfeit peace and joy. In fact, it is our fear and concern over losing "things" or "position in life" or relationships that causes

12

us to forfeit peace and joy. It is in giving all things into His hands, and letting go, that we find true inner peace. "Thy will be done Lord." If we are born again and heaven bound, then everything that happens to us between now and heaven is for our good. Everything! We need to believe this and act like God knows what He is doing with our lives. Romans 8:28 states, "And we know that all things work together for good to them that love God, to them who are the called according to his purpose." And what is that purpose? It is stated in the next verse, "For whom he did foreknow, he also did predestinate to be conformed to the image of his Son." This conforming to the image of Jesus is the result of the pressures and challenges that refine our responses until we learn to respond in all things as Jesus would.

Satan wants to rob the Christian of joy. He does this by attempting to cause us to look at the testing, look at the problems, and focus on them rather than on the inner work of the Holy Spirit. As we learn to welcome challenges and problems as God's refining hand, we defeat the devil and enter the joy of the Lord in the midst of our sometimes unpleasant circumstances. Our joy does not come by God changing our circumstances, or changing the people in our life we find difficult. That is Satan's lie. It is the evil one who attempts to get us into a mind set of, "if I only had this or that I would have joy." Or, "if this thing or that thing in my life would just change or go away, then I would have joy and peace." These things are simply not true. Joy does not come from the changing of outward matters, but from inner yielding to the light of God's Word and learning to respond like Jesus. We need to say in the face of all difficulties, "I am a blood-washed saint of God, I am heaven bound, God is in control of my life, and I will stand in my faith in Him in the midst of my current circumstances, whether they change or not, for my joy is to do the will of my Father." (See Hab.3:17-19.) Then we can stand ready to receive the joy and blessing of God! Don't entertain Satan's bait that things and outward change bring joy. This is the lie the world is chasing after and it bears no spiritual fruit. God is always looking at how we react in situations. The situations themselves are only tools in God's hands. When we have mastered an inner issue, the situation will change to take us to the next level. We should not expect our refining to be over so soon. There is yet a lot of work for God to accomplish in each of us.

If we blame circumstances for our unhappiness, we have listened to the devil. Our unhappiness is most often a result of disobedience to God. (Though we experience sorrow and grief, we need not forfeit inner peace and joy.) Somewhere we have not yielded to His will. Somewhere we have taken matters into our own hands, to do our own will, to protect ourselves, or accomplish our own desires apart from Him. It is never our circumstance that is our problem, it is our inner attitude toward our circumstance. It is not other people that rob us of joy, it is Satan, as we listen to the flesh and self-will rather than the Holy Spirit. In the garden, Eve blamed the serpent for beguiling her. Adam blamed Eve for giving him the fruit. God held each of them responsible for their own sins. Satan may be the one beguiling us to look at our circumstances and think that by changing them, or other people, we would be happy; but, it is our individual responsibility to resist his lies and obey God anyway. We have no one to blame for a lack of peace and joy but ourselves. If we obey God, we will be blessed, and that is certain. There is nothing that can take our joy or peace when we have entered there through the door of obedience.

If we join the devil and the flesh with "poor me, nothing ever goes right for me" type thinking, then we rob ourselves of God's blessing. We need to do what God says, "Be careful for nothing, but in every thing by prayer and supplication with thanksgiving, let your requests be made known unto God" (Phil. 4:6). Which then continues, "and the peace of God, which passeth all understanding, shall keep your hearts and minds through Christ Jesus." The peace and joy the angels were so excited about is the peace and joy that comes from obeying God, thanking Him in all things, loving our enemies, praying for those that hurt us, becoming like Jesus in the inner man of the heart. Our circumstances matter nothing when we are right with God on the inside. Paul praised Him in prison.

Are we unhappy? Are there people that seem to ruin our lives? Are there circumstances in our life we just can't stand? Praise God! If we will learn to praise and thank Him for the testings, we will begin to find the secret path to inner joy and peace. When our heart's response becomes one with the Holy Spirit, and we are loving and gracious in the face of adversity and difficult situations because we have chosen to die to the flesh that would react apart from God, then not only peace and joy are ours, but the power of God becomes activated on our behalf to bless, protect, help, and lift us up. No wonder the angels were excited!

2

YIELDING YET MORE

Heavenly Father, purge us of all remnants of the flesh, and self will, which plague us and keep us from a deeper relationship with You. Purify our motives in the deep and secret places of the heart. Let us obey the Holy Spirit in every moment of life, and quickly restore us when we stumble over our old man of sin. Kindle a fire of diligence and obedience within our hearts that we may please You. Glorify Your name in the earth, and grant us the determination and strength to pay the price of obedience. In Jesus name we pray. Amen.

"WHO MADE ME A JUDGE OR A DIVIDER OVER YOU?" (Luke 12:14)

In Luke 12, Jesus was approached by a man with a request for help. He had a situation which, to him, seemed unfair. His brother had received control over an inheritance to which this man thought he had a rightful share. What a shock it must have been when his brother gained control over the inheritance and would not share it. No wonder he felt to seek the help of the Lord in this matter. We know how we would feel if someone took something of ours, something we had every right to have, and "robbed" us of our ability to possess or have it.

If we unfairly lost money, a source of income, a piece of real estate, a car, or other items which were ours, we too might seek God's intervention in the matter. So we read, "And one of the company said unto him, Master, speak to my brother, that he divide the inheritance with me" (Luke 12:13). If this was our request, we would hope and expect the Lord to say, "bring Me to your brother, and I will straighten him out, and correct his selfishness." But this was not the Lord's response. Jesus said to him, "Man, who made me a judge or a divider over you?" (Luke 12:14). This was probably a greater shock than the first. Was Jesus supporting the greedy brothers actions?

Such a response would, and should, stop us cold to consider what is wrong. "Why is God so harsh toward me when I am within my rights? Those things I asked for are mine. What is going on here anyway?" Jesus was speaking the only way he could to this man, because the man's inner heart attitude toward the inheritance was incorrect. He had not yielded the matter to God, but rather was seeking God to help him in his own effort to keep something he did not want to lose. The man's heart was coveting after the inheritance. Yes, it was due him. And yes, his brother may have been wrong to not share it. However, Jesus was working in this man's heart to perfect the inner man of the Spirit. Jesus wants every corner of the believer's heart to be yielded to Him, and He uses all of life's experiences to accomplish that work.

The Scripture tells us that "ye are not your own. For ye are bought with a price: therefore glorify God in your body, and in your spirit, which are God's" (I Cor. 6:19-20). If we are not our own, then nothing we may possess in this life is ours either. We must learn to yield all things to Him in order to receive His blessings. Our reward is not in seeking self rights, but in yielding self rights to God and trusting Him for our blessing and reward. This is not easy, but it is necessary if we wish to receive His blessings. If we seek to use the name of the Lord to protect our self rights, then we misunderstand His Lordship and have fallen into being controlled by the flesh and the devil. In I Cor. 6:7, Paul says to those who were going to the law to get matters settled for their own self rights, "Now therefore there is utterly a fault among you, because ye go to law one with another. Why do ye not rather take wrong? why do ye not rather suffer yourselves to be defrauded?" Peter reinforces the same heart attitude in I Peter 2:19-23, saying that Jesus committed himself to God when mistreated, trusting God to deal with the offender and the offended. Standing up for ourselves is a heart attitude that is difficult to let go of, but one we must learn to yield to the Spirit's control.

Jesus then, following this man's errant request for recovery of the inheritance, brought forth several teachings on covetousness. By the time He got through, this man must have felt about three inches tall, and had hopefully repented of a wrong heart attitude. Jesus taught that it was foolish to be rich in this world, but not rich toward

God. This man was seeking to maintain his worldly riches, but Jesus saw that he was lacking in spiritual riches (Luke 12:16-21). He proclaimed that when God is sought first, and the heart is yielding all things to Him, that God would provide and add to a person's life all the blessings that the world is busy seeking (Luke 12:22-32). God would have given the man who lost a portion of the inheritance much more, had the man placed obedience to God first, yielded his painful losses to heaven's control, and pressed on with his walk with Jesus. (Mark 10:30.)

Jesus gives an insightful warning in Luke 12:58, saying, "when thou goest with thine adversary to the magistrate, as thou art in the way, give diligence that thou mayest be delivered from him; lest he hale thee to the judge, and the judge deliver thee to the officer, and the officer cast thee into prison." In other words, when our flesh, self-will, and seeking self rights (our adversary, and the adversary of the Holy Spirit) seeks to gain control of our hearts and actions, we are best served to quickly seek deliverance from such wrong thinking or we will be cast into the prison of our own self-controlled darkness, until we repent and seek God's help and forgiveness. The Bible teaches us that vengeance belongs to the Lord, and that He will repay, as written in Romans 12:19: "Dearly beloved, avenge not yourselves [don't seek self rights], but rather give place unto wrath: for it is written, Vengeance is mine; I will repay, saith the Lord." He continues with an admonition to not be all caught up in anger toward those who wrong us or take from us, for in so doing we would be overcome with evil ourselves, the evil of a wrong and vengeful heart. "Therefore if thine enemy hunger, feed him; if he thirst, give him drink: for in so doing thou shalt heap coals of fire on his head. Be not overcome of evil, but overcome evil with good" (verse 20-21).

And now we can see why Jesus responded as He did. The wronged man should have prayed, "Lord, You see what my brother has done. I come to You and lift the matter into Your hands. Inheritance or not, I am here to serve You and live for You. Make my heart right in this matter, and draw my brother closer to You. Keep me from coveting after worldly things, and help me release control of this and all things into Your hands. Forgive me for any wrong, bitter, or angry thoughts toward my brother. Thank You that You are my provision and source of life and blessing." May we be granted grace to learn to respond in ways pleasing to God in all matters, and to quickly turn from the adversary of the flesh that would tell us, with Satan's prompting, to take matters into our own hands. Jesus seeks to empty us of self so that our lives may be an even brighter light in this world. As we learn to yield to the Spirit in all of the secret areas of the heart, then we will become as Jesus spoke in Luke 11:36: "If thy whole body therefore be full of light, having no part dark, [no self seeking left] the whole shall be full of light, as when the bright shining of a candle doth give thee light."

3

AVOIDING THE UNPLEASANT...
WHY IT DOESN'T WORK!

Heavenly Father, we bow before You with grateful hearts. We take this moment to thank You for Your love and mercy which has so graciously given us the gift of life. Our sins are forgiven and washed completely by the blood of Jesus. Our hope is renewed daily in the face of every challenge. While fear and uncertainty may flood the hearts of many, yet we stand sure in our trust in You and the promises of Your Word. Words cannot tell how thankful we are to be known by You, and called to be Your children. May we learn to praise and thank You even more for Your great love toward us. In Jesus' name we pray. Amen.

"JESUS PREVENTED HIM" (Matt. 17:25)

As we live our lives in this world, we are often faced with a moral dilemma, an ethical challenge, or some situation which will test our character and spiritual convictions. We will be called upon to give an answer, or make a decision, regarding a matter which our Lord is observing. We may not consciously consider that He is watching, but He always watches. Peter faced just such a moment when he was questioned, "Doth not your master pay tribute?" (Matt. 17:24). Peter didn't know quite how to handle the question. He quickly said "yes", and dismissed the matter.

Peter did not wish to deal with the responsibility of paying tribute, and presumed an answer of yes would avoid any difficulty. He would quickly learn that seeking to avoid an issue does not work, particularly with those upon whom the Lord has placed His hand.

When Peter then entered the house where Jesus was, Jesus stopped him and asked a question about tribute and custom. We read, "And when he was come into the house, Jesus prevented him, saying, What thinkest thou, Simon? of whom do the kings of the earth take custom or tribute: of their own children, or of strangers?" There it was again! The issue which Peter had just dismissed moments earlier was brought before his face again, by the Lord. Jesus had observed Peters actions, had found them needing some instruction and improvement, and had immediately brought the matter up with Peter. The wording "prevented him" is particularly important as we ponder the actions of Jesus. The Lord will prevent us from moving forward from issues He brings before us, until we learn what God desires. He will bring them before us repeatedly, until we listen to His instruction and take the appropriate action.

Following Jesus' "preventing" Peter, the Lord required Peter to go out and take the necessary action to correct the situation. He required Peter to do the thing which he should have done in the first place, and that was to pay the tribute. We read, "Notwithstanding, lest we should offend them, go thou to the sea, and cast an hook, and take up the fish that first comes up; and when thou hast opened his mouth, thou shalt find a piece of money: that take, and give unto them for me and thee" (Matt. 17:27). It would have been easier for Peter to pay the first time. Often, if we mishandle something once, there is more involved in correcting our actions the second time – a walk to the sea, time spent fishing, and then paying the tribute. Seeking to avoid matters which God intends for us to handle only complicates the ultimate solution.

And then there is the lesson of faith, which the Lord packaged into Peter's instructions. A fish's mouth is not normally where one would look to pay a debt. With somewhat of a sense of humor, Jesus teaches Peter, "plan to do the right thing, don't avoid responsibility, and I will make a way for you and provide for you." And He did.

Is there a place where we find Jesus "preventing" us? Standing in the way and calling our attention to a matter we need to address? If so, we are wise to deal with it quickly, as procrastination will only make things more difficult. As we step in the direction of doing the right thing in the sight of God, we can trust in His help, provision, and strength.

I WILL STAND

I will stand,
Though the winds may blow o'er my soul,
I will stand and know that His power,
Is greater than
Anything, that comes against me,
And that in Him is my victory.

I will put my trust in Him
As my faith is purified, by the fire
Of the trials that come.
I will stand, and see His love,
I will stand, and see His salvation.

I will praise His holy name,
When I cannot see the way,
For I know, that by faith I stand
And that I am loved by Him
Who died, Who died, for me.

I will see His salvation,
See His salvation,
As I stand,
He will come,
And I will know His love.

(Lyrics by Lex Adams)

GOD WANTS A RELATIONSHIP!

Heavenly Father, we are in constant need of divine light by which to see and learn from the circumstances and events of life. We cheapen the glorious sacrifice of Christ on the cross by wrongly applying our own untransformed thinking and energy to the holy work of the Spirit. You sent your Son to die for us. He willingly sacrificed Himself to purchase our salvation, and to cause us to know You personally. Establishing the relationship between God the Father and many believing children individually, for eternity, was accomplished on the cross. Forgive us for tarnishing this great purpose with efforts born out of any source other than that relationship with the Spirit you died and bled to give us. Grant that our focus may be on knowing You, obeying You, and yielding to You. And if any activity is commenced, grant that it be born out of the Spirit and our relationship with You, not our lower untransformed nature. In Jesus' name we pray. Amen.

'NOT EVERYONE WHO SAITH UNTO ME, LORD, LORD, SHALL ENTER INTO THE KINGDOM OF HEAVEN." (Matt. 7:21)

These words of Jesus can be troubling, and they should be. They should cause us to think seriously about where we stand in light of our eternal salvation, and to examine closely our works (or that which we believe to be works) for the Lord. Jesus said that calling upon Him as Lord is insufficient to purchase our eternal salvation. He stated that heaven is reserved for those who do the will of the Father, which is in heaven. Heaven's purposes are to be manifest in our lives now, as we live daily, as this proves that we belong to Him and are heaven bound. We cannot get there by our works, but our lives should bear out the works of heaven if we are doing the will of God.

Jesus acknowledges that many are confused and will remain so until heaven escapes them. They will die not having come to understand the will of the Father. They will have missed their precious chance to know God and eternal life. And these of which he spoke were not the blatant unbelievers and outwardly sinful, but rather the religious, the doers of good things. He says, "Many will say to me in that day, Lord, Lord, have we not prophesied in thy name? and in thy name have cast out devils? and in thy name done many wonderful works?" (Matt. 7:22). These words are amazing to our religious lower nature. We wrestle with them as to argue with God, reasoning, "you mean I can preach about God, do spiritual works, and be involved in many good works toward mankind, for my church, and for the world, and yet miss heaven?" Yes! This is precisely Jesus' point. The Lord's answer to this argument was simple and profound. "And then will I profess unto them, *I never knew you*: depart from me, ye that work iniquity" (Matt. 7:23). We must never let ourselves be confused as to God's purpose...*relationship!* What is our relationship with Him? How well do we know Him personally? Are we getting to know Him better in our pilgrimage through life, or are we too busy with good activity to allow Him intimate entrance into our lives?

Jesus cuts straight to the heart of the confusion. Religious activity is nothing, relationship is everything. Any good that comes from the life of a Christian comes as a result of a personal relationship with Jesus, not from noble efforts to do good or religious things. This is the problem with too many of us today. We are motivated to religious action to somehow justify ourselves before God. We derive a sense of release from guilt and justification that we are godly by works rather than relationship. Even those who have begun to know Him and are heaven bound may yet enter the ranks of the confused by replacing yielding and obedience with religious activity. Paul spoke to the Galatians admonishing, "Are ye so foolish, having begun in the Spirit, are ye now made perfect by the flesh?" (Gal. 3:3). Once we are introduced to Jesus by the Holy Spirit, we must remain on the Spirit's course, which is focused on causing us to know God the Father better. It is a message of darkness which promotes activity outside of God Himself. God is never the one pushing us into activity. He is drawing us to come to know Him better, so that we may behold the works which He desires to accomplish. There is a great difference between religious activity and knowing God.

If we never come to know Jesus on a personal level, our soul will suffer eternal torment. If we do know Him and launch out into activity without Him, or seek to substitute religious works for yielding and obedience to Him, we will suffer the loss of even the works we think we have accomplished. (I Cor. 3:11-15.)

We by nature are not very good at sitting still. It is easier to be doing things than to deepen our relationship with God. We are easily thrown out of focus with God's priorities. To make us one with Him, to mold us into His likeness that we might know Him, these are God's priorities. What are ours? To build and do great things? To achieve a sense of accomplishment? Or are we willing to let our own energies be pressed through the cross until we have none of our own and are fit for God's purposes? There is great joy in the common places of life when we can learn to see the work of God there.

Jesus declared "I never knew you, depart from me." As we see that He desires for us to know Him, we can better understand His displeasure with our activities which stand in the way of our relationship with Him. May we learn to say "depart from me" to all efforts of self which keep us from a deeper relationship with Jesus. Wrongly sourced activity may give us a sense of appeasing God or self-satisfaction that we are okay with God, but only obedience and knowing Him will bring lasting peace and joy. When our focus is correct, we can find great joy in the most unspiritual settings, for we find Him there.

Conversely, death and rejection are to be found in the greatest of religious works if He does not know them. Relationship is everything to the Father. The Son sacrificed Himself to spiritually introduce us to the Father. The price paid emphasizes the importance to God. We are wise to ponder and learn the will of the Father. Does He know us? Does He know our works, that is, are they born of our relationship with Him through the prompting of the Holy Spirit?

5

PRAISE HIM CONTINUALLY AND BE BLESSED!

Heavenly Father, we pause to take time to praise and thank You. Too often we plead our case before You, are blessed by Your answer and help, and neglect to offer the praise and thanksgiving due You. May we no longer neglect to continue to praise and thank you for all things. Your kindness toward us is unceasing. Your blessings abound in our lives. And through each and every challenge You have kept us, taught us, and led us to a place of greater understanding and peace. Praise and bless Your holy name today and forever! In Jesus name we pray. Amen.

"OH THAT MEN WOULD PRAISE THE LORD FOR HIS GOODNESS" (Psalms 107:15)

Psalm 107 ends with this verse, "Whoso is wise, and will observe these things, even they shall understand the loving kindness of the Lord." Let us look at the message in this Psalm, that we may be encouraged by God's loving help toward people with many faults and problems such as our own, and learn of the Lord's ways and lovingkindness. The first 7 verses tell of a time when God's people wandered in the wilderness alone, finding no city in which to dwell. They were hungry, thirsty, and discouraged. We read "...their soul fainted in them. Then they cried unto the Lord in their trouble, and he delivered them out of their distresses. He led them forth by the right way, that they might have a city of habitation." He heard them, and His lovingkindness moved Him to help them when they called. In all of our challenges, as we call upon the Lord, He will likewise help us. The psalmist then writes in verse 8, "Oh that men would praise the Lord for his goodness, and for his wonderful works to the children of men!"

Verses 9-14 speak of the Lord "satisfying the longing soul" and "filling the hungry soul with goodness." Those who were in great affliction because of rebellion toward God, even those He showed mercy and "brought out of the darkness and the shadow of death, and brake their bands in sunder." He saved – even the rebellious out of distress when they cried unto Him. We may have many flaws and weaknesses, yet as we bring them to Jesus and ask His help, He will not refuse to answer our prayers. He will not stop helping us because of our imperfection. He will help us in our imperfection, as we acknowledge it and call upon His name. The Psalmist then repeats, "Oh that men would praise the Lord for his goodness, and for his wonderful works to the children of men."

Verses 16-20 speak of fools being in affliction because of their transgressions, and coming near to death because of their sin. Yet when they cried unto the Lord He sent and delivered them from their destructions. It is comforting to see that foolish actions or words do not permanently cut us off from the Lord's help. (The Lord knows we have all made enough of them!) Again we read the repeated message, "Oh that men would praise the Lord for his goodness, and for his wonderful works to the children of men!"

We then read of those who make a living at sea, in the great ships. David says that these men know the works of God first hand. We read, "For he commandeth, and raiseth the stormy wind, which lifteth up the waves thereof. They reel to and fro, and stagger like a drunken man, and are at their wits end. Then they cry unto the Lord in their trouble, and he bringeth them out of their distresses. He maketh the storm a calm, so that the waves thereof are still. Then are they glad because they be quiet; so he bringeth them unto their desired haven" (Psalm 107:25-30). Our storms may not be at sea, but they may be just as distressing. He is with us in them in whatever form they may take. This example is followed again by, "Oh that men would praise the Lord for his goodness, and for his wonderful works to the children of men!"

David then continues to extol the greatness and kindness of God saying, "He turneth rivers into a wilderness, and the watersprings into dry ground; a fruitful land into barrenness, for the wickedness of them that dwell therein" (Psalm 107:33-34). God has power to humble the wicked and proud in many ways, including altering our surroundings, and not through nature alone. We then read, "He turneth the wilderness into a standing water, and dry ground into watersprings. And there he maketh the hungry to dwell, that they may prepare a city for habitation; and sow the fields, and plant vineyards, which may yield fruits of increase. He blesseth them also, so that they are multiplied greatly; and suffereth not their cattle to decrease" (Psalm 107:35-38). God makes a way when there seems to be none! He takes the needy, the hungry, the foolish, the rebellious, the distressed, and all others who cry unto Him, and blesses them. He overlooks the weakness and faults of our lives, and hears only our cry. Wherever we have been, when we stop and turn to call upon God, in the name of Jesus, His loving-kindness will move Him to help! How glorious!

In every example which David wrote, God came to help and deliver those who called upon Him. And four times David pleaded, "Oh that men would praise the Lord for his goodness, and for his wonderful works to the children of men!" We cry unto the Lord often and with great effort when we are distressed. He answers in His loving-kindness and mercy. However, do we continue to praise Him and thank Him unceasingly for His goodness and His works of kindness toward us? It is the plea of this psalm that we would. For it is in praise and gratefulness that we are drawn nearer to Him. It is in praise and thanksgiving that we grow in His likeness and are positively influenced by His Spirit. Of the ten lepers healed by Jesus, in Luke 17:11-19, only one returned to praise and glorify God. David observed something similar, for he pleaded repeatedly that men would learn to praise and thank God for His goodness and His works toward men. If we taste of wisdom and understand the loving-kindness of God, we cannot help but praise and thank Him continually. It is in learning to praise Him when blessed, as well as when challenged that we find the richest blessings of God upon our hearts.

6

ENVY...RECOGNIZE IT!
AVOID IT!

Heavenly Father, we seek to have Your mind in all things. Our thinking is in need of a complete overhaul in so many areas. Wash us and free us from the limited perception of our own minds, and renew our thoughts with the light of Your understanding. As we see things the way You see them, then we find peace, victory, and endurance. Our assurance of Your nearness comes not from the removal of difficulty, but from Your insight enlightening our thinking. As we trust in You and learn Your purposes, then we can rejoice in Your presence always and in all things. We are grateful and thankful for Your Spirit, Your love, and Your constant never-ceasing care for us. Thank You that we are loved by Him who died for us, and rose again for our salvation. In Jesus' name we pray. Amen.

"TRULY GOD IS GOOD TO ISRAEL" (Psalm 73:1)

David speaks of a great enlightenment to his thinking in Psalm 73. He says "Truly God is good to Israel, even to such as are of a clean heart." This was what he learned, that truly God is good to His people, even though at times things may appear out of balance. David acknowledges that his thinking was affected wrongly by what he perceived to be the inequity of God. Things which David beheld were "out of balance" in his mind. God was blessing the wicked while harassing the righteous, or so David thought. David says, "For I was envious at the foolish, when I saw the prosperity of the wicked...they are not in trouble as other men; neither are they plagued like other men" (Psalm 73:2-5). This observation was troubling to David, for in his own life he was constantly challenged, chastened, and under the corrective hand of God. He says in verse 14, "For all the day long have I been plagued, and chastened every morning." David saw the foolish and wicked appearing to prosper with a free hand and no correction from God, while he was constantly (every morning) being chastened by the Lord. It seemed wrong, out of balance, unfair. Attempting to understand this apparent inequity was painful for David, it tormented him. (verse 16.)

In Verse 2, David realized that such thinking was dangerous to his walk and standing with God. He learned that this type of thinking would cause him to slip and fall. Fall into what? Into bitterness of heart, resentment harbored inside that would poison all of David's actions, his witness and his ministry. We need to guard our hearts from any inner seeds of envy, anger, bitterness, or resentment, for they will cut us off from seeing God and understanding His ways. This is Satan's ploy to damage the Christian, for it is we who suffer from wrong heart attitudes, not those of whom we are envious or hold bitterness toward. It is never what happens to us, or what we see happening in the lives of others that is important, it is our inner heart attitude that God seeks to correct and perfect. When David drew near to God and consulted with the Lord, then he learned to think correctly on these matters. We read in verse 17, "Until I went into the sanctuary of God; then understood I their end." Where there is no chastening from the Lord, there is the development of evil thinking and attitudes. Left untended, wickedness grows like weeds in a garden. Chastening purges the unwanted weeds and prunes the growth of the good plants. Verse 5 states that the wicked were not in trouble as other men. Verses 6-9 explain the results of such apparent ease: "Therefore pride compasseth them about as a chain; violence covereth them as a garment. Their eyes stand out with fatness: they have more than heart could wish. They are corrupt, and speak wickedly concerning oppression: they speak loftily. They set their mouth against the heavens, and their tongue walketh through the earth." Left to themselves, they continue in a path of wickedness and darkness. They may appear to prosper, but only for the moment, for as David explains, their end is not pleasant. David saw their ultimate failure and wrote in verses 18-20, "Surely thou didst set them in slippery places: thou castedst them down into destruction. How are they brought into desolation, as in a moment! they are utterly consumed with terrors. As a dream when one awaketh; so, O Lord, when thou awakest, thou shalt despise their image."

The wickedness of man is purged by the chastening hand of God. Where there is no chastening, there is no growth and no increase of light. Psalm 73 is David's realization of what we read in Hebrews 12:5-8: "My son, despise not thou the chastening of the Lord, nor faint when thou art rebuked of him: for whom the Lord loveth he chasteneth, and scourgeth every son whom he receiveth. If ye endure chastening, God dealeth with you as with sons; for what son is he whom the father chasteneth not? But if ye be without chastisement, whereof all are partakers, then are ye bastards, and not sons." Prosperity without the chastisement of God may appear good, but it is empty and only a temporary step on the road to destruction.

Prior to understanding these things, David entertained the thought, "Verily I have cleansed my heart in vain" (Psalm 73:13), as he watched the wicked proceed unscathed. It didn't seem fair to David. He was seeking to please God, and yet watched as others who rejected God's ways seemed to prosper and never suffer unfairly. At times, David was challenged, not because of any wrong doing on his part but by God's allowing things which would help in his growth. We read in Psalm 59 of David being threatened by evil men for doing nothing wrong himself: "For, lo, they lie in wait for my soul: the mighty are gathered against me; not for my transgression, nor for my sin, O Lord. They run and prepare themselves without my fault..." (verses 3-4). When looked at without the enlightenment of God, such testing can bring us perilously close to the place of falling of which David spoke in the second verse of Psalm 73. After seeing the truth, David repented, saying, "If I say, I will speak thus; behold,

I should offend against the generation of thy people," and "Thus my heart was grieved, and I was pricked in my reins. So foolish was I, and ignorant: I was as a beast before thee." David acknowledges that his former thinking of enviousness for the prosperity of the wicked was no better than the thinking of an ignorant animal – unenlightened, foolish, and offensive. God's caring efforts, working His great love toward His people through His daily chastening, correcting, and helping (in the realm of things eternal and invisible) would be counted as worthless by such base thinking. David was deeply convicted of his error. He realized that "whom the Lord loveth He chasteneth!" (Heb. 12:6).

Then, in verses 23-28 David summarizes wisely. Turning his eyes away from the prosperity of others, and fixing his gaze upon His Lord he writes: "Nevertheless I am continually with thee: thou hast holden me by my right hand. Thou shalt guide me with thy counsel, and afterward receive me to glory. Whom have I in heaven but thee? and there is none upon earth that I desire beside thee. My flesh and my heart faileth: but God is the strength of my heart, and my portion for ever. For, lo, they that are far from thee shall perish: thou hast destroyed all them that go a whoring from thee. But it is good for me to draw near to God: I have put my trust in the Lord God, that I may declare all thy works." We can say nothing else except "God is truly good to me", as we know and stand in the fact that we are loved by Him, in every circumstance.

FINDING JOY
IN OUR TRIALS

Heavenly Father, thank You for your faithfulness. Your answer to prayer is amazing, as we see Your love and caring revealed toward us each day. Your Word is a rock upon which we may stand and never fall. Your arms are outstretched to uphold us in each moment of trial and testing. Your power is manifest for our benefit and protection as we navigate the challenges of life with our eyes upon You. Give us patience, peace, and strength of faith, that we may glorify You in the face of adversity, challenge, and uncertainty. Lord, men's hearts shall fail them for the things that come to pass around us. May our hearts be strengthened to bring light and hope in the midst of such darkness. In Jesus' name we pray. Amen.

"THAT THE TRIAL OF YOUR FAITH...MAY BE FOUND UNTO PRAISE" (I Peter 1:7)

There are seasons to our walk and relationship with the Lord. Some are harsh, as the bitter cold of winter. Some are refreshing, as the warmth and fragrance of spring. At times, we feel the prolonged heat of summer, wishing for one cooler day. And the transition of fall is beautiful, though it signals the coming of yet another winter season. Peter speaks of being in a season of heaviness through manifold temptations (I Peter 1:6). This being a time of testing, as he further explains. Later, in I Peter 4:12, Peter speaks a caring reminder to the believer, saying "Beloved, think it not strange concerning the fiery trial which is to try you, as though some strange thing happened unto you." This reminder needs to be spoken often, for we sometimes forget that the seasons change, and that we will most likely face many a winter season before the end of our journey. We may be fresh from the wonders of a spring, summer and fall in our walk with Jesus, but yet another winter will come our way.

There is a deepening work of transformation which the Holy Spirit seeks to accomplish in each heart cleansed by the blood of the Lamb and purchased of God. Faith is a precious thing which God seeks to refine and perfect as we come through many different experiences in this life. I Peter 1:5 reads: "Who are kept by the power of God through faith unto salvation..." In all seasons, in all hardships, in all times of blessing, we are kept by the power of God, through faith, unto a purposed end planned by God – our salvation, our inheritance in eternity. We are *kept*, by *faith!* In the midst of the testing, we are kept. We are not left alone. We are not abandoned to the strength of the circumstance or left to be crushed by the challenge. We are kept! Though the winds may seem to blow us off course and threaten our safety, yet we are kept and guided through each and every challenge as our faith is exercised to praise and trust the Lord.

Difficulties can cause us heaviness. We feel the reality of the pain of sickness, the worry of finances, the concern for loved ones, the anxiety of concern over many things which touch our

42

lives. Faith doesn't necessarily take the heaviness away, but we will be kept through it, lifted above it and shown the love and provisions of God as we place our trust in Him. We will be brought through it, into the planned blessings of God. We will not be left "forsaken", even though we may feel that way at times. "Some strange thing" touching our lives may not be what we expected in our walk with Jesus, but to Him it is not strange, it is a tool of refining, a hand of divine love, seeking to make us more into the image of Jesus than we were before. "That the trial of your faith, being much more precious than of gold that perisheth, though it be tried with fire, might be found unto praise and honour and glory at the appearing of Jesus Christ" (I Peter 1:7). It takes the "fire" of circumstances to prepare our hearts for the refining work of the Spirit of God. We must be softened by the heat in order to be molded by His hand. The impurities of our hearts are removed by His love as we seem to be melted by the heat of the trials. Just as gold is heated to be purified and shaped.

In the heat of God's transforming fire, claim that you indeed are kept by the power of God. Claim it in the midst of the worst of circumstances. Stand in faith upon the promises of God's Word. Take them as your own, for they are His gift to you. As we learn to see difficulty as His refining of our faith, then we gain great insight into the purposes of His work in our inner life and the outer circumstance loses its power to destroy. Yes, it may try us. Yes, it may feel heavy and dark. But it cannot destroy us, for we are kept by the power of God through faith.

We must not let the enemy destroy our faith. Peter admonishes us to "gird up the loins of your mind, be sober, and hope to the end..." (I Peter 1:13). Hope right on through the trials of faith, hope to the *end*. An absolute determination to trust Him is a clear manifestation of the finest purification of our faith. In Chapter 4 he continues, "forasmuch then as Christ hath suffered for us in the flesh, arm yourselves likewise with the same mind:" This mind set will help us to remember to not think it strange when we are tested.

Peter speaks in I Peter 1:6 of two distinctly opposite emotions taking place at the same time in our walk with Jesus – rejoicing and heaviness. This is healthy, for it depicts a soul that is rejoicing over the salvation of God and the nearness of the Holy Spirit, while at the same time being heavy over what is being experienced here on earth to accomplish God's deeper work in our hearts. This is the proper perspective which will enable us to come through the testings refined and strengthened, not destroyed. It is an attitude of faith which proclaims: I am focused upon and have accepted as mine, the great promise of God's love and eternal salvation through Jesus Christ. Come what may on my journey to eternity, I will rejoice in that promise. I will rejoice in His presence with me each day, though I suffer through many testings for the time being. I rejoice, for in all things, and through all things, I am kept by the power and love of God. This is the refining of faith which will be found to glorify the Lord at His coming!

8

LEARN TO STAND IN THE MIDST OF UNBELIEVING OPINIONS

Heavenly Father, we come to You to be touched by the life-changing power only You possess. We cannot make ourselves better in Your sight. The mere exercising of diligence in the skills and gifts given does not mean we have grown thereby. The successes we may experience in the world do not always equate to growth in the Spirit. All the experiences we pass through will only help to make us into Your likeness if we yield and learn the precious lessons You have placed in them. Help us discover the treasures you desire us to find in the many differing settings of our lives. Let our focus be on those things of eternal value, and grant us wisdom to know where to place our priorities. At the end of the day, may we look up to see that we have yielded to Your gentle promptings, shunned the temptations to yield to the flesh, yielded to be a good witness in our actions and words, and left behind some fragrance of Your gracious presence. In Jesus' name we pray, Amen.

"THEY AGREED NOT AMONG THEMSELVES"
(Acts 28:25)

Upon Paul's arrival in Rome as a prisoner he called the chief Jews together to speak with them about his captivity and why he had appealed to Caesar. As he spoke to them, they said that no letters had been sent to them regarding Paul, nor had any of the brethren spoken anything about him. They did acknowledge they had heard about Paul's "sect" and they understood it to be evil-spoken of everywhere. They went on to say they wanted to hear what Paul had to say about his beliefs. They were curious, intrigued, or even perhaps genuinely interested to learn of the preaching of Jesus. Following this first meeting with Paul, the Jewish leaders arranged a day for Paul to speak to them (Acts 28:16-23).

Upon the appointed day, a good number of people came to Paul's place of residence to hear him speak. All day long, Paul spoke to them about Jesus and demonstrated from Scripture how Jesus was the Christ. He gave them clear examples from the law of Moses and the writings of the prophets. At the end of the day we are told in verse 24, "and some believed the things which were spoken, and some believed not." The preaching of the Gospel will more times than not have a similar result, some will believe and some will not. What happened next is where every soul needs to exercise caution. The good received from the Word of God can be destroyed quickly if we are not prepared for this likely subsequent event. Discussion! Discussion with the hope of reaching agreement with others, or support for our position from others.

Following Paul's teaching of the message of Jesus as Savior, we are told that "some believed...and some believed not." Then we read, "when they agreed not among themselves, they departed." A time of discussion took place between those who believed and those who did not. Doubt and unbelief were poured over the hearts of those who did believe from the mouths of those who did not. The resistance of the non-believers seemed to carry the day, for Paul's closing words to the entire group were, "Well spake the Holy Ghost by Esaias the prophet unto our fathers, saying, go unto this people, and say, hearing ye shall hear, and shall not understand; and seeing ye shall see, and not perceive: For the heart of this people is waxed gross, and their ears are dull of hearing, and their eyes have they closed; lest they should be converted, and I should heal them. Be it known therefore unto you, that the salvation of God is sent unto the Gentiles, and that they will hear it."

We then read, after Paul had spoken these last words of rebuke, "the Jews departed, and had great reasoning among themselves." What is to be learned from this passage of Scripture? Simply, reason not with others about what God is speaking to your own heart. Take your questions and reasoning to God Himself. Search out the Scriptures for yourself and trust God to clarify any confusion through prayer and patient waiting upon Him. Do not seek to find support among friends and family. They may not be open to the things of God. The Spirit works on each heart individually. If many are touched, it is because they were individually ministered to by God. Those who receive not the things of the Spirit cannot be looked to for consensus. The group of Jews in Acts 28 left the gathering in disagreement and in a state of great reasoning. They did not leave standing firmly upon the truth that was shared by Paul.

In Matthew 13, Jesus gives us the parable of the sower. In this parable we see several different results upon the hearts of those who heard the word of God. In verses 19-23 we see that some people hear the word and do not understand it. The wicked one then comes and takes away that which was sown. The result is the word is not received, nor believed. Others hear and believe for awhile, but when difficulty comes because of their belief they abandon their faith. Others believe, yet become too involved in other desires and are unfruitful in their lives. Yet others hear the word and believe, and continue in their faith. If you were to put together a group of people from each category described in the parable, it is highly doubtful you could reach a consensus of agreement among them. Those who did not understand the word would cast a shadow over the faith of the others. Those who had abandoned their faith would likely seek to justify their position. Those who were new in their faith could be affected by the unbelief of the others. The result would probably be similar to what Paul observed among the Jews in Acts 28. To be in a state of "great reasoning" and disagreement is not profitable for the soul.

We need to be aware of this trap and seek to work out our own salvation with the Savior, not with the others in our lives. Has God quickened His truth to your heart? Then trust in that work of the Spirit and seek to grow through study of the Word and prayer. Do not be discouraged if others don't share what God has shown you. Keep them in your prayers, but do not let unbelief quench the work of the Spirit in your own heart, regardless of the source of the opposition.

9

CUTTING THE ROPES OF
SELF CONFIDENCE

Heavenly Father, help us to trust You more. Cause us to understand the benefit of releasing all things into Your control. Our efforts are ineffective and feeble by comparison to Yours. That which we would manipulate for our benefit would be a greater blessing if left to You. You have our best at heart. Thank You and praise You for Your great care toward us. The thoughts You think toward us are thoughts of goodness and blessing. It is a good thing to learn of our own helplessness, for then we look more to You and rely more upon Your mercy and love. Teach us Your ways, that we may walk in the light of Your understanding in each of our daily challenges. In Jesus' name we pray. Amen.

"CUT OFF THE ROPES...AND LET HER FALL AWAY." (Acts 27:32)

Paul, after serving the Lord for many years, was taken prisoner and was being sent to Rome because he had appealed to Caesar following the Jews' accusations against him. Aboard a ship in the custody of a centurion named Julius, Paul found himself completely in the control of others. He had no say on when and where the ship would sail. Although he had admonished them not to risk the ship, for he perceived the sailing to be dangerous

(Acts 27:9-11). His advice was rejected and Paul was compelled to sail into a fate he perceived to be hazardous. He had no choice.

Shortly thereafter, the ship encountered a severe storm. In Acts 27:18-20 we read: "And we being exceedingly tossed with a tempest, the next day they lightened the ship; and the third day we cast out with our own hands the tackling of the ship. And when neither sun nor stars in many days appeared, and no small tempest lay on us, all hope that we should be saved was then taken away." Paul, having warned them not to sail, being a prisoner with no options, captive against his will, was with them in this dire situation. And so was the Lord! Paul stood and spoke to all aboard, "Sirs, ye should have hearkened unto me, and not have loosed from Crete, and to have gained this harm and loss. And now I exhort you to be of good cheer: for there shall be no loss of any man's life among you, but of the ship. For there stood by me this night the angel of God, whose I am, and whom I serve, saying, Fear not, Paul; thou must be brought before Caesar: and, lo, God hath given thee all them that sail with thee. Wherefore, sirs, be of good cheer: for I believe God, that it shall be even as it was told me. Howbeit we must be cast upon a certain island" (Acts 27:21-26).

In appearance, Paul was the captive being taken on this journey by the centurion and in the control of the captain of the ship. In God's eyes, all the others were sailing with Paul, for the angel of God said to him, "God hath given thee all them that sail with thee." God was keeping Paul and granting protection to all around him, even though they did not heed sound advice and were most probably ignorant of the Lord. Nothing is capable of separating us from the love and protection of the Lord! Certainly, circumstances beyond our control are well within the control of God!

As the ship, after 14 nights at sea, began to approach land, the crew set anchors, fearing they would hit rocks in the dark of the night if they ventured too close to shore. (Acts 27:27-29.) Then, seeking to save themselves, the crew attempted to flee the main ship in the smaller boat on board. Paul warned that if the crew left, the rest aboard, including the soldiers, could not be saved. At this warning, the soldiers cut the ropes and let the boat fall away into the stormy sea. There was now no means of escape from the ship. All would share in the fate which lay ahead. This last little boat could well have represented the last possible way for any of the men to save themselves. They now were cast upon the mercies of God alone, with no other options. Frankly, this is not a bad place to be! I wonder how often we seek to escape a situation by lowering our "life boat" into the sea for fear of what may come? Perhaps a better approach is to "cut off the ropes of the boat, and let her fall off." To have nothing of ourselves left to rely upon, and wait patiently upon the Lord, is a sure place of peace and ultimate victory.

Having no way of escape, Paul spoke to the men to encourage them to eat, and again promised that "there shall not an hair fall from the head of any of you." They then waited for the light of day to make an attempt to sail closer to land. The ship ran aground and began to be broken in pieces, so into the sea went every soul. Those who could swim did so, and those who could not held onto pieces of the ship to float. We then read in Acts 27:44, "And so it came to pass, that they escaped all safe to land."

As the events unfolded, there were times of uncertainty and hopelessness. Lives were threatened. Just before leaping into the sea to swim for land, the soldiers wanted to kill the prisoners, including Paul. God intervened and caused the centurion to keep the soldiers from killing the prisoners, for he wished to save Paul. At each step, God spoke to Paul to comfort him and help in the situation, or moved others in order to accomplish His purposes. This was a rough journey. Fourteen days at sea in a severe storm, the loss of the ship, and the threatened loss of life. The beauty of the story is the faithfulness of God to His people regardless of the journey! Blessing and provision do not always come in a package of serenity and calm. Here, in the midst of a storm, we find God dispensing hope, guidance, encouragement, and ultimately deliverance from the danger. It was messy, difficult, and stressful, but it was a journey He was aware of and one He took with Paul. He will take our difficult journeys with us also.

10

TRUST IN THE UNSEEN
THINGS OF GOD

Heavenly Father, You are kind and understanding beyond what we deserve. We are grateful for Your guidance, faithfulness, and generosity toward us. We falter all too often in the challenges presented to us. Grant us grace and strength to better respond to the winds of life, which blow against our souls. Preserve our faith until the day of Thy soon coming. Gird us with determination to do Thy will alone. May our time, each moment of it, be spent to further Your desires here on earth. In Jesus' name we pray. Amen.

WEANING THE SOUL IN PREPARATION FOR THE HOLY SPIRIT

Following the devastating crucifixion and burial of the Lord Jesus, the believers He left behind struggled with the events that had so rapidly transpired. They had experienced, in just a few days, the miracle working power of His presence, His "trial" and crucifixion, and his burial. Then, when they went to the grave with spices, He was gone! As two of them walked and communed on the road to Emmaus, He joined in their discussions. They were confused. They thought He would have redeemed Israel, which had not happened (Luke 24:21). He was missing from His grave and was reported to be alive

(Luke 24:23). After Jesus responded and explained the Scriptures to them, they recognized Him, but then He disappeared. As they rushed to tell the apostles, Jesus Himself joined them again. Their response was, "they were terrified and affrighted, and supposed that they had seen a spirit" (Luke 24:37).

Jesus spent considerable time convincing them He was indeed the risen Lord. He showed them His hands and feet, and shared food with them. We are told "then opened He their understanding, that they might understand the scriptures" (Luke 24:45). The concept of the death and resurrection of Christ was difficult for even His closest followers. They struggled with it. In Luke 24:50-51, we read that Jesus was then taken up from them into heaven. However, this was not immediately after first reappearing to them. (At that point they were in no shape to be left alone as His messengers!) The event took place 40 days later! For over a month following His resurrection, and prior to His final ascent into heaven, Jesus spent time with His disciples. In Acts 1:3 we read, "To whom also he shewed himself alive after his passion by many infallible proofs, being seen of them forty days, and speaking of the things pertaining to the kingdom of God." Verse 2 refers to these disciples as being the apostles. It took more than one appearance of Jesus to establish in these men what God desired. Jesus worked with them for 40 days getting them prepared for what lay ahead. He also instructed them, as we read in Acts 1:4, "commanded them that they should not depart from Jerusalem, but wait for the promise of the Father, which, saith he, ye have heard of me. For John truly baptized with water, but ye shall be baptized with the Holy Ghost not many days hence." Jesus was preparing them to move into the realm of the unseen. He would be gone from visual sight, but the Holy Spirit would come to them. The Holy Spirit of God would empower them, teach them, lead them, and guide them. This was the plan all along! To reunite lost man to God directly, one on one, through the Spirit of God coming into man. As the Spirit had been in Jesus, so now He was to be in every believer.

Between His first appearance to the apostles, and being taken up to heaven, Jesus confirmed His resurrection to this group by "many infallible proofs." He would not leave it to just one brief meeting. He worked to be sure they understood the depth of what had happened. By repeated confirmation, He wanted them totally convinced of the events and their meaning. Then would they be unwavering to move in the power of the Holy Spirit who was being sent to them from the Father after Jesus' departure. We do not read of any Jewish non-believers being upset about His presence during these 40 days. His appearance was to those who believed, not the world in general. (The rulers of the Jews seem to have been completely blind to these appearances.)

There was also another motive in Jesus' frequent appearances to his disciples. As He seems to have made appearances to them, and then disappeared from them for periods of time, (Luke 24:31 & John 21:1), it was as though He was weaning them from relying upon His visual "flesh and bone" person. He wanted their faith to be in the unseen realm of God the Father. The more he appeared again and again, resulting in the summation of "many infallible proofs", Jesus established their faith in preparation for the ministry of the Holy Spirit. By His frequent appearing, they gained a comfort that indeed He was nearby, always. (See John 20:19-31 and John 21:1-14.)

Jesus knew the ministry of the Holy Spirit would require this "weaning" from His physical presence. He had to prepare them for His departure. Even the angels gently admonished them to stop gazing into Heaven, after His ascension, as He would one day return (Acts 1:10-11). How kind is our God in His dealing with us! Those of us who have believed without having been in His "flesh and bone" presence, have been brought directly into the relationship God planned. By believing in Jesus as Savior, upon the hearing of His Word, we were "born again" into the family of God in the Spirit. However, we may still need some weaning experiences. We yet need our eyes trained to focus upon Him in the realm of the unseen, and not falter into trusting in the things seen. Is there something in our lives we look to more than to Jesus? If there is, God will work to wean us from our dependencies also. God will be as gentle with us as with the apostles, if our heart's desire is to yield our will to Him and draw closer to Him. When all we see is vanished, and we stand before God, will our faith have been in Him alone? If all were taken from us tomorrow, are we confident in our standing with the Lord? If the answer is yes, then we are at least partially weaned from trusting in things other than Jesus.

When we trust in God in the Spirit, we move in the same way Jesus did. What He suffered from unbelief and misunderstanding, we will suffer. As His followers began preaching salvation through faith in the name of Jesus, then were the non-believers riled to persecute the disciples of Christ. The mantle had been shifted, from Jesus to His followers. They were now the messengers! They were moving in His power, and receiving the attacks from the enemy of light. Jesus knew His disciples would need their faith strengthened in the things of God not seen in the natural. They had to learn to be confident in His nearness, though not visible, and they required the power of the Baptism of the Holy Spirit to be victorious. So do we!

SAFETY IN THE MIDST OF DANGER

Heavenly Father, we thank You that You will finish the good work You have begun within us. It is Your work, Lord, and we are grateful as You continue to minister to us by giving us more understanding into Your ways. Your Word is full of more treasures than a lifetime can discover. Thank You for the Holy Spirit who comes to help us as we seek You. Continue to give us greater light in those areas where we do not see clearly. Quicken to us the truth which strengthens us in challenging situations, brings us joy in all things, and brings us peace as we rest in Your care. Forgive us for our ignorance and lack of faith. Mold us into Your own image Lord, by the inner work of Your Spirit. In Jesus' name we pray. Amen.

"BUT HE PASSING THROUGH THE MIDST OF THEM WENT HIS WAY." (Luke 4:30)

Following the temptations of the Lord described in Luke 4:1-13, Jesus "returned in the power of the Spirit into Galilee: and there went out a fame of him through all the region round about. And he taught in their synagogues, being glorified of all" (Luke 4:14-15). Jesus began to be received of many as He taught and ministered to the people. The Holy Spirits' anointing rested upon Him. As He taught, people were deeply touched, so much so that a "fame of Him" spread throughout the region. Then we read that He came to Nazareth, the area where He had been raised. Here he proceeded into the synagogue, as He was accustomed to doing, and stood up to read. He read, "the Spirit of the Lord is upon me, because he hath anointed me to preach the gospel to the poor; he hath sent me to heal the brokenhearted, and to preach deliverance to the captives, and recovering of sight to the blind, to set at liberty them that are bruised, to preach the acceptable year of the Lord." As He sat down, every eye was upon Him. The way He had spoken, quickened by the Spirit, had caught their attention. He told them, "this day is this scripture fulfilled in your ears." And we read that "all bear him witness, and wondered at the gracious words which proceeded out of his mouth." But then we read of their doubt and confusion as they asked one another, "Is not this Joseph's son?"

Though they bore witness in their hearts, their minds and unbelief blinded them to His ministry. They saw only "Joseph's son," not the Son of God. Jesus then gave them two examples from the Scriptures of when God chose not to minister to the people of Israel, but rather to foreigners. The comparison was made to demonstrate that in times past, unbelief had prevented God's children from receiving God's blessing, guidance, and correction through God's prophets. The same unbelief that was now preventing them from receiving what Jesus would give them. Jesus told the story of the widow woman who lived in Sidon, and had been fed by the Lord as she provided shelter for Elijah. God sent Elijah there for his protection and provision rather than to any widow in Israel. At the time, Israel was under the rule of king Ahab, a man who had turned his back on God and caused Israel to sin greatly. Elijah had foretold of a drought, which brought hard times to Israel, and Ahab sought after Elijah, blaming him for the drought and Israel's troubles. God chose to send Elijah to this *foreigner's* home to provide for him, as well as the widow.

Next, Jesus told of the healing of Naaman, a Syrian in the days of Elisha. Jesus explained that there were many lepers in Israel at this time, but none had been healed, only Naaman, and he was a Syrian. The king of Israel thought that Naaman's request for healing was a provocation, so strange was it to his ears. Elijah said, send him to me and he shall know there is a prophet in Israel. (II Kings 5:8) From these examples we could conclude that Jesus was showing them that the power of God had been present in those times, but Israel had not sought God to be healed, or to be helped in the famine. Or, their hearts were not right, and thus they were prevented from receiving His help and blessing. God was present to heal Naaman, who came to Israel seeking to be healed. God provided for the widow woman and Elijah in the midst of the famine, and God healed her son when he became sick (I Kings 17). Jesus infers that Elijah and Elisha were not honored in their own country, and that God blessed those who did receive them, though they were not Jews. "Verily I say unto you, no prophet is accepted in his own country" (Luke 4:24). Jesus was revealing their unbelief to them, using these past examples, and they resented Him for doing so.

Upon hearing Jesus' words, the people in the synagogue in Nazareth, "were filled with wrath, and rose up, and thrust him out of the city, and led him unto the brow of the hill whereon their city was built, that they might cast him down headlong" (Luke 4:28-29). They were greatly offended by the words of Jesus. He had accused them of not honoring God's prophets. He had said that by not receiving His words they were rejecting God's messenger. They refused to accept that. They were correct in their own eyes, and "Joseph's son" was not going to reprimand them. Unbelief and hardness of heart prevented them from receiving God's blessing through Jesus.

An angry crowd dragged the Lord out of the synagogue and out to the edge of the hill on which their city was built. They intended to throw Him down head first. This was a violent crowd, and the Lord was being swept away with their anger and malice. They had taken hold of Him and dragged Him to within moments of being cast down the hill. Then we read: "But he passing through the midst of them went his way" (Luke 4:30). Somehow, God caused this mob to lose control of Jesus. He did not lift Jesus out of the angry crowd. He did not sweep Him away in the Spirit. Simply, God caused Jesus to be free from their ill intentions, and so He walked "through the midst of them." This is a beautiful message! Right in the middle of a very adverse experience, God made a way for Jesus to go "His way"! The might of the crowd was powerless. A path was made right through the adversity, not by being removed from it.

There is no adversity, challenge, or difficulty through which the Lord will not make a way for those whose eyes and faith are focused upon Him. The surrounding difficulty may not change, but through it God will make a way! There is no power capable of keeping us from going "His way" as our faith is placed in Him. There may be times when we come close to the "edge of the hill of destruction," but we can believe God to make a way even then! Elijah was safe in the widows home, and was fed in the midst of the famine. Jesus was safe in the midst of the angry crowd. We are in His hands *always*, without exception, and in this we can rejoice.

12

THE HAZARDS OF PRIDE

Heavenly Father, we bow before You, for You alone are worthy of our praise and adoration. We cannot count the ways You have helped us. We are amazed at Your attentiveness to our prayers and needs. You do not need to be so merciful and caring toward us, for we have done nothing to deserve Your love, yet You love us. For this we are grateful. Grant that we may never turn from seeking Your face, Lord, especially in times of blessing and rest. Testings have a way of throwing us into Your arms, while times of rest tend to find us lazy. Kindle a fresh fire of desire to seek You, and to yield to Your purposes in our lives. In Jesus' name we pray. Amen.

"HIS HEART WAS LIFTED UP: THEREFORE THERE WAS WRATH UPON HIM." (II Chronicles 32:25)

It is difficult to walk in the blessings of the Lord. Difficult because it is easy for us to fall into thinking too highly of ourselves. Some of the greatest kings of Israel fell from a godly heart attitude after years of dedication to God. Three of them were Solomon, Josiah, and Hezekiah. They started their rule humble and broken before the Lord, served Him without compromise, only to later fall into difficulty. While the reasons vary, the fact remains: even the greatest of God's servants may fall if their heart attitude ceases to be broken and contrite. We must never lose sight of our deep need for God's help, even after years of receiving His assistance.

Hezekiah's story is amazing. His strength and commitment to God were exceptional. In II Kings 18-20 and II Chronicles 29-32, we read of Hezekiah's life. Early in his reign, he sought to destroy all the things which hindered Judah from following the Lord. He even destroyed the brass serpent which Moses had made. For years, the children of Israel had burned incense unto it. No king before him had even recognized the idolatry in this. Hezekiah did! (II Kings 18:4).

Following years of rule by an evil king, Hezekiah repaired the house of the Lord. Upon reopening it and establishing the order of sacrifice and offering, he wrote letters to all Israel for them to come to Jerusalem to keep the Passover unto the Lord. While he was laughed to scorn by most, many came and were blessed as they again followed the commandment of God (II Chron. 30:10). "So there was great joy in Jerusalem" (II Chron. 30:26). After this, there was a cleansing of the land as the people went out and "brake the images in pieces, and cut down the groves, and threw down the high places and the altars" (II Chron. 31:1). In all that Hezekiah did, he set his heart to please God, "and in every work that he began in the service of the house of God, and in the law, and in the commandments, to seek his God, he did it with his heart, and prospered" (II Chron. 31:21).

Following his good works for God, Hezekiah faced a severe challenge. [*Commitment and dedication spare none of us from the testing and refining hand of God.*] The king of Assyria came to fight against Jerusalem. Hezekiah's faith was tested as the enemy shouted accusations against God and Hezekiah to all who could hear them on the walls of Jerusalem. Threatening letters were also sent. In this hour of despair, Hezekiah, and Isaiah the prophet, prayed and cried out to the Lord. At the hearing of the threat, we are told that Hezekiah, "went into the house of the Lord." Upon receiving the letter, he also, "went up into the house of the Lord, and spread it before the Lord." It was this constant reliance upon God that prospered Hezekiah, even in the face of destruction. God answered the prayers of Hezekiah and Isaiah, and sent an angel to destroy the leaders of the enemy army (II Chron. 32:1-22). After these events, many began to greatly look up to Hezekiah. We read, "and many brought gifts unto the Lord to Jerusalem, and presents to Hezekiah king of Judah: so that he was magnified in the sight of all nations from thenceforth" (II Chron. 32:23). Perhaps this was the beginning of Hezekiah's difficulty. Being praised by others can cause the heart to rise from its knees, ceasing to be humble and contrite.

In II Kings chapter 20, we read of the healing of Hezekiah, and God's miraculous sign to him to assure him of his healing. The sun moved backward ten degrees in the middle of the day! It was after this healing, that

Hezekiah responded unwisely to letters from the prince of Babylon, who had written, "to enquire of the wonder that was done in the land." We are told that "God left him, (Hezekiah) to try him, that he might know all that was in his heart" (II Chron. 32:31). Hezekiah proceeded to receive the Babylonian visitors, and show them the wonders of his treasures (II Kings 20:13). He "boasted of his blessings", which were the gifts of God, and showed them off to the rulers of Babylon. Hezekiah did not respond well to the praises and acknowledgement he received from the prince of Babylon. He bowed to it, and his heart was lifted up improperly in the sight of God. Isaiah was then sent to reprove Hezekiah (II Kings 20:14-19). II Chron. 32:25 summarizes: "But Hezekiah rendered not again according to the benefit done unto him; for his heart was lifted up: therefore there was wrath upon him, and upon Judah and Jerusalem."

We rejoice, when on our knees we humble ourselves, beseech God and find His help. We need to exercise caution when we are praised of others, even for God's blessings. It can too easily lead to wrong actions and reproof from God, if our hearts are lifted up. Jesus did not submit Himself to the praises of man, for we read: "Now when he was in Jerusalem at the passover, in the feast day, many believed in his name, when they saw the miracles which he did. But Jesus did not commit himself unto them, because he knew all men, and needed not that any should testify of man: for he knew what was in man" (John 2:23-25). Care is constantly required to give God *all* of the praise and glory!

Hezekiah was first dedicated. Then his faith was tried, and he was humbled by the testings of an enemy invasion. Then he was lifted up in his own eyes by his victory and healing. And finally, again he was humbled by the words of Isaiah. (II Chron. 32:26) The lifting up came with the victory and healing. Humility came with reproof and testings. Testing, trials, and reproof can all yield the desired result – humility – if we yield our hearts to Him. Caution must be exercised in the times of blessing and victory!

13

AVOID UNNECESSARY TROUBLE

Heavenly Father, we rejoice in Your wonderful works. Barriers formed by wrong thinking, roots of sin which cause great difficulty, and our inability to see the source of the devastation, are healed, released and corrected in the blink of an eye as Your Spirit ministers to our hearts to set us free. We pray for Your continued help in keeping us from the sin and trouble caused by our resistance. Grant us grace to release those things, and relationships, we are not meant to control. For by refusing to do so, we hinder our relationship with You and others. Hasten Your good work in us Lord, for as we look back upon past enlightenments, we desire to be helped in the areas we do not yet understand. It is Your great love which seeks to liberate us fully from the chains of sin which bind our hearts with wrong attitudes and thinking. We admit our great ignorance. We ask for Your continued help. In Jesus' name we pray. Amen.

"WHEREFORE LET HIM THAT THINKETH HE STANDETH TAKE HEED LEST HE FALL." (I Cor. 10:12)

In the tenth chapter of I Corinthians we are told an important fact concerning our reading and learning from the Old Testament writings. We read: "Now all these things happened unto them for ensamples: and they are written for our admonition..." (I Cor. 10:11). We can learn from the triumphs and mistakes of those who have gone before us. Our understanding is enriched as we ponder the matters discussed and observe the actions of the people and the response of God. Today, our battles may not be in mortal combat and the kingdom we seek to protect may not be a vast land. More likely our battles are matters which touch our personal lives relating to family, work, ministry, and ourselves. The kingdom we seek to protect is a right heart attitude. It is the stance in the heart that is central in the stories of the Old Testament. While the scene of the events may be quite different than that of our personal lives, yet the lessons to be learned are the same.

In II Chronicles: 34 & 35, we read of the life of King Josiah. He was only eight years old when he began to reign. We are told: "And he did that which was right in the sight of the Lord, and walked in the ways of David his father, and declined neither to the right hand, nor to the left" (II Chron. 34:2). When he was twenty-six, he committed to repair the house of the Lord. In the process, the book of the law of the Lord, given by Moses was found. As it was read to the king, he realized great wrath was promised to come upon the people because of their sins and their turning away from the Lord. Josiah set his heart to seek the Lord and sent a delegation to inquire of Huldah, the prophetess. We read: "And Hilkiah, and they that the king had appointed, went to Huldah the prophetess, the wife of Shallum the son of Tikvath, the son of Hasrah, keeper of the wardrobe;...and she answered them, Thus saith the Lord God of Israel, Tell ye the man that sent you to me, Thus saith the Lord, Behold, I will bring evil upon this place, and upon the inhabitants thereof, even all the curses that are written in the book which they have read before the king of Judah: because they have forsaken me, and have burned incense unto other gods, that they might provoke me to anger with all the works of their hands; therefore my wrath shall be poured out upon this place, and shall not be quenched. And as for the king of Judah, who sent you to enquire of the Lord, so shall ye say unto him, thus saith the Lord God of Israel concerning the words which thou hast heard; because thine heart was tender, and thou didst humble thyself before God, when thou heardest his words against this place, and against the inhabitants thereof, and humbledst thyself before me, and didst rend thy clothes, and weep before me; I have even heard thee also, saith the Lord. Behold, I will gather thee to thy fathers, and thou shalt be gathered to thy grave in peace, neither shall thine eyes see all the evil that I will bring upon this place, and upon the inhabitants of the same" (II Chron. 34:22-28). God was moved to assist this young king because of his humble and sincere heart attitude.

Josiah continued to follow the Lord, as we read: "And Josiah took away all the abominations out of all the countries that pertained to the children of Israel, and made all that were present in Israel to serve, even to serve the Lord their God. And all his days they departed not from following the Lord, the God of their fathers" (II Chron. 34:33). They also observed the Passover feast at Josiah's direction. It was said that there was no such Passover kept since the days of Samuel the prophet (II Chron. 35:18).

Josiah was a man whose heart was set to follow God. As a result, many turned their hearts to the Lord during Josiah's life. After the wonderful and correct things which Josiah had done, and the tremendous zeal he had for the Lord, the king of Egypt came up to fight against Charchemish, by the Euphrates. He did not come to fight with Josiah nor Judah. Nevertheless, Josiah decided to go and fight against the king of Egypt. Necho, king of Egypt, sent ambassadors to Josiah saying, "what have I to do with thee, thou king of Judah? I come not against thee this day, but against the house wherewith I have war: for God commanded me to make haste: forbear thee from meddling with God, who is with me, that he destroy thee not. Nevertheless Josiah would not turn his face from him, but disguised himself, that he might fight with him, and hearkened not unto the words of Necho from the mouth of God, and came to fight in the valley of Megiddo" (II Chron. 35:20-22).

Josiah did not seek the counsel of God over this matter. He was stubborn in his insistence to fight the king of Egypt. Although concerned enough to disguise himself in the battle, his hiding did not protect him. As a result, he lost his life in the battle at a very young age. We read: "And the archers shot at king Josiah; and the king said to his servants, Have me away; for I am sore wounded...and they brought him to Jerusalem, and he died" (II Chron. 35:23-24). We also will find no protection behind a disguise of our heart's deepest motives. God looks beneath our best disguises, to heal us of any wrong underlying motive. Where there is destruction, there is likely an insistence upon our own will. As we ponder the admonition in I Corinthians 10, we see the value of such advice: "let him that thinketh he standeth take heed lest he fall." All of the good we may have done in the past will not keep us from the consequences of a wrong heart attitude today. If we take upon ourselves a thinking which does not rely upon the Lord in every moment for guidance and protection, we are vulnerable to defeat and difficulty. God helped Josiah when his heart was "tender, and he humbled himself before God." When his heart was lifted up in a battle God did not want him to fight, God left him to his own destruction. [II Chron. 35:22 discloses that the admonition for Josiah not to fight was from the mouth of God.]

May the Lord help us not take into our own pride His acts of mercy, help, victory, provision, and protection. *Humble* and *tender* is where our hearts will find the power and blessing of God.

14

UNYIELDING THOUGHT PATTERNS, ROBBERS OF GOD'S BLESSING

Heavenly Father, we seek Thy face to learn to know Thee better. We are comforted by the life found in Your Word. We are nourished by its truth. Our minds are conformed a little more to Thy ways each time we ponder the wonders of the Bible. Your message to us is one of love, forgiveness, restoration, and life. While we deserve none of these, yet we are grateful for Your care and great love toward us. Open our understanding more and more, for we see so very little. We have no offerings to give Thee that are comparable to Your love and to Jesus' sacrifice. So we come to give You our lives, our hearts, our wills, our days. Take them and make them meaningful to Thee, and somehow useful in the work of Your kingdom. Glorify Thy wondrous name through our vessels of clay. In Jesus' name we pray. Amen.

A GLIMPSE INTO THE WAYS OF THE SPIRIT

The story of the healing of Naaman, the captain of the host of Syria, is an intriguing view of several aspects of the ways of God. It begins with a raid by Syria on Israel in which an Israeli maid is captured and becomes a servant to Naaman's wife. Through this maid's word of testimony about God being able to heal leprosy, Naaman comes to the king of Israel with a letter from the king of Syria asking him to heal Naaman's leprosy. Naaman had responded with faith to the words of his wife's servant girl, prepared himself for the journey to Israel, and went expecting to be healed. This word of testimony from a captured slave girl was to turn a powerful leader in Syria into a believer in the living God. "Would God my lord (Naaman) were with the prophet that is in Samaria, for he would recover him of his leprosy" (II Kings 5:3).

Although the king of Israel displayed no faith and was threatened by the request to heal Naaman, yet the prophet Elisha responded with faith and confidence in God. Elisha sent to the king of Israel and said, "Wherefore hast thou rent thy clothes? Let him come now to me, and he shall know that there is a prophet in Israel" (II Kings 5:8). So Naaman was sent to Elisha.

Naaman was a man of war. He was a mighty man of great authority in the land of Syria. He arrived in front of Elisha's house with his horses, chariot, and servants. Presumptuously he expected Elisha to greet him with regard to who he was, and perform a dramatic act to heal him. Elisha did nothing of the sort. He quietly sent a messenger to speak to Naaman. He didn't even come out to meet him. Elisha was not desirous of being acknowledged of himself, he was obeying God, and God was desirous of Naaman acknowledging Him, not Elisha. The messenger said, "Go and wash in Jordan seven times, and thy flesh shall come again to thee, and thou shalt be clean." Naaman was enraged! He charged away in his chariot to leave in great anger. God and the prophet had not met Naaman's preconceived ideas. This was not how Naaman had envisioned being healed. He resisted God's direction because it seemed foreign to his own thinking. We read: "Naaman was wroth, and went away, and said, Behold, I thought he will surely come out to me, and stand, and call on the name of the Lord his God, and strike his hand over the place, and recover the leper. Are not Abana and Pharpar, rivers of Damascus, better than all the waters of Israel? May I not wash in them, and be clean? So he turned and went away in a rage" (II Kings 5:11-12). There is a great lesson in this error. We too easily turn from the guidance of the Spirit, because we cannot fit it into our own thoughts and ways. Our pride can cause us to stumble at this point. We come perilously close to losing His blessing when we respond in this way.

Naaman was then spoken to by his servants who convinced him to do as the prophet had said. They reasoned with him and said, "If the prophet had bid thee do some great thing, wouldest thou not have done it? How much rather then, when he saith to thee, Wash, and be clean?" We then read that Naaman goes to Jordan. Looking at the water, he must have wondered, "what difference will this make, it is but water?" It was humbling for him to step down from his chariot, disrobe, and submerse himself in the water, with his servants watching. It was not a great noble act. It was not "some great thing" as his servants had said. He stepped into the water once and got out. He repeated this seven times. It took faith to do this seven times. After the sixth time he looked at his flesh and still he was a leper. He could have stopped, but he didn't. One more time he entered the water, and upon coming out he looked at his body. His servants were watching also, and there before his eyes his flesh turned clean and new again, like the flesh of a child. Imagine the feeling in Naaman's heart. He had obeyed, humbled himself, and overcome his pride and anger. He had stooped to submerse himself seven times in the river Jordan. He was cleansed and healed.

Naaman then returned to Elisha and proclaimed, "Behold, now I know that there is no God in all the earth, but in Israel" (II Kings 5:15). Further he said, "Thy servant will henceforth offer neither burnt offering, nor sacrifice unto other gods, but unto the Lord." Naaman had met God. Elisha had handled the situation as God had required and not thrust himself between Naaman and the work God was doing in Naaman's heart. The Spirit had done the work from beginning to end. From the word of testimony from the captive slave girl, to the instructions of Elisha, to the humbling of Naaman, and the healing of the leprosy, God had directed, and God was glorified. Thus by allowing the Spirit to direct, many were blessed along the way. Naaman returned home a believer in the God of Israel. We are not told what effect this had upon those around him, but we do know that they saw him leave as a leper and return healed. This was known by all those around him in his home country, including the king of Syria. Jesus even references this healing as he revealed the unbelief in those to whom he was speaking in Nazareth (Luke 4:27). The power of faith and obedience is far-reaching. Whatever our role may be, may we seek to be obedient and responsive to the ways of His Spirit.

15

DON'T GIVE UP BECAUSE OF THE APPEARANCE OF THINGS

Heavenly Father, we are grateful to You for Your love and care. We are awakened to the reality of Your presence daily, as we stop to consider how we are blessed. The power of Your Word is beyond compare! Its working in our lives is revealed in the most unlikely of situations, yes, in all situations. From all that is written, we are given a wealth of examples which we see unfolding within the setting of our own lives. There can be no doubt, You will never leave nor forsake us, for we see You manifest in our lives daily. In the difficult situations, in our testings, in our victories, in our uncertainty, we see You in them all, even if sometimes later than You would desire. Forgive us for our lack of faith, and our doubt which blinds us to the working of Your sacred hand in our life. Open our eyes anew to the wondrous presence of the Holy Spirit in each moment. For it is only as we trust Thee by faith, that we can walk in Thy peace. In Jesus' name we pray. Amen.

"THEY THAT BE WITH US ARE MORE THAN THEY THAT BE WITH THEM." (II Kings 6:16)

King David was a man who was confronted with many battles, challenges, and tribulations. His life was not one of quietude. In his old age he spoke a wonderful statement of his observations about God's care for his people. He spoke from a platform of a lifetime of experiences and relationship with God. He said, "I have been young, and now am old; yet have I not seen the righteous forsaken, nor his seed begging bread" (Psalms 37:25). The righteous are not left alone, they have the companionship of God! The book of Hebrews confirms these words saying, "I will never leave thee, nor forsake thee" (Hebrews 13:5). This is absolute fact! God will not leave those who have been born again!

This promise is an anchor for our souls. Trials and difficulties will of necessity come. There will be a multitude of experiences we each will pass through. We will fight our own battles as did David. We will struggle to understand God's plan and purpose in the midst of many things. There are times when it will be hid from us, for a season. This does not mean we are forsaken. This does not mean God has withdrawn His love for us. Faith must grow. Our trust in God must be blind to what surrounds us. We must **know** that our God is with us always. We must simply **know** this! And we learn to know this as David did, by looking back and seeing that we have been preserved through our past challenges. We have been sustained by His unseen hand which has brought us to this day. He has been there all along. God has answered prayer, sometimes slowly (by our judgement), sometimes rapidly. We can look back and see He has been there, behind the scenes, when at the moment He was invisible and seemingly distant. As our faith and trust are matured, He is never invisible. We know He is there regardless of what we are facing.

There is a wonderful story, in II Kings chapter 6, of two men facing an overwhelming enemy. One had his eyes of faith open, the other did not – at first. Elisha was sought by the king of Syria because he was warning the king of Israel of Syria's military strategy. God was telling Elisha what to tell the king of Israel for Israel's protection. Finally, the king of Syria found the city where Elisha and his servant were located. One night, the king of Syria's army surrounded the city. When Elisha's servant rose early in the morning and went outside, he saw the host of Syria surrounding the city with chariots, horses, and a great host. He returned to Elisha and said, "Alas, my master! how shall we do?" Alas indeed! What a hopeless looking situation. Where would they run? How could they escape? The appearance of the matter was disastrous.

Elisha answered his servant: "Fear not: for they that be with us are more than they that be with them." Where was this *more* of which Elisha spoke? The servant certainly did not see them. One man (Elisha) saw victory and resources to help, and his servant saw only the host of Syria standing against him and his master. The servant saw a hopeless situation. Elisha saw God! Elisha then prayed as we read in verse 17: "Lord, I pray thee, open his eyes, that he may see. And the Lord opened the eyes of the young man; and he saw: and behold, the mountain was full of horses and chariots of fire round about Elisha." God was there all the time, visible to Elisha, yet not visible to his servant until his eyes were opened in the spirit. Elisha then prayed for God to blind the entire army of Syria, which the Lord did. The balance of the story is rather humorous, as two men, Elisha and his servant, lead the entire army of Syria captive to the king of Israel. God delivered Elisha from this hopeless appearing situation because of his faith and trust in God.

Are we surrounded by an enemy army in our lives? Is there an attack being made upon us by Satanic forces? Is there a circle of hopelessness appearing to close us in? **God is with us!** Let us pray to see His help, and let us trust and exercise our faith in His presence in our lives. These accounts of God's help are given to us for our edification and to sustain us in times of challenge. As we release our faith in God and His written Word, we will see the armies that assail us led away captive as God preserves us unto the day of His coming. And may the Lord help us to remember, that though the afflictions of the righteous may be many, He promises to deliver us from them all! (Psalms 34:19). Praise God!

16

FACE IT AND BE BLESSED...
WE HAVE NO EXCUSE FOR OUR SIN

Heavenly Father, we come before You once again
and lay aside the guilt of our shortcomings and sin. We
let go of it, for holding onto our guilt only separates us
from You in our own minds. You stand ready to accept
us always, even the instant after we falter, provided we
confess our sins and place our hearts afresh beneath
the cleansing blood of Jesus. It is Satan that would lie
to us and deny us fellowship with You. Therefore, we
come! We come in weakness. We come with imperfections. We come with pains and distress. We come not
seeing all things clearly. But Father, we come, for in
You alone are the answers, the comfort, and the words
of eternal life. Work out in our daily lives Your purposes. Let us not be as the one who looks into Your
face, but then turns to daily life forgetting what we are
to be in Thee. Keep us in a walk in the Spirit, that our
lives might be a light and encouragement to those
around us. In Jesus' name we pray. Amen.

"SO THEN EVERY ONE OF US SHALL GIVE
ACCOUNT OF HIMSELF." (Romans 14:12)

Accountability of one's own life and actions is clearly
defined in Scripture. The fact that there is a day of judgment
in which each man will give an account and answer for

his actions is also clear. "For we must all appear before the judgment seat of Christ; that every one may receive the things done in his body, according to that he hath done, whether it be good or bad" (II Cor. 5:10). (See also Rev. 20:12.) Romans 14:12 makes a very important point about accountability. We will each give account of ourselves. We will not give account for the others who touch our lives. There is a school of thought which says, "people have problems because of how others have raised or treated them." A broken home is the reason for juvenile crime and gangs. Single parents raise more troubled children than married couples. Abusive spouses are the product of being raised in abusive homes. Such thinking gives the person in the gang or the abusive spouse an excuse for their problem. If this logic holds true of itself, then, on the day of judgment, the thief will say, "Lord, it is my parent's fault, for they divorced when I was young and I therefore got into trouble. Don't judge me for my actions, judge them for failing me." Scripture does not support this outcome. The thief will be judged for stealing. The abusive spouse will be judged for his or her own actions, with little regard for the particular excuse for such behavior. Being a victim is not justification for sinful behavior.

The root problem is not how we are raised or treated by others, nor what behavior we observe. The root problem is the fact we are born in sin. Our sinful nature will take us down one wrong road or another until we are yielded to God and transformed by the power of the indwelling Holy Spirit of God. The fact that wrong behavior by others affects us is true. But it is not a valid excuse for sinful behavior. Each parent will give an account of their works as parents. Each spouse will give account of how they treated their spouse. Each person will give an account of the example they were to others. Wrong actions by anyone will have an evil effect on others. This evil effect is not license for sin. God is able to transform any person who comes to Him. I do not speak to justify or minimize wrong actions. There is no doubt that they have a significant effect on other people. An abusive parent creates a very great challenge for any child to overcome. But whether our challenge is an abusive parent, an unfair employer, or wrongful imprisonment such as Joseph endured, we still must individually stand before Christ and answer for ourselves what we have done with His message of salvation. What has the troubled child done with the message of Jesus Christ? What has the ill-behaving individual done with the message of God's deliverance and transforming power? The purpose of this chapter is to strip us of all excuses. We have none! Yes, the road has been rough. Yes, we have been wronged. Yes, we could justify our behavior in our own eyes, and perhaps in the eyes of certain others as well. Yes, our parents, and we as parents, have made mistakes that affected us and others. Before God, we have no excuse. We are commanded to yield to Him and the work of His Spirit in our hearts (James 4:7-8, and Romans 12:1-2). I Peter 2:18-23 speaks beautifully to this issue.

The challenge is to accept accountability *today* for our own actions. Some of us may have faced greater obstacles to overcome, but regardless of the size of the unfair or cruel things that have touched us and shaped us, we must throw them aside as invalid excuses and today walk in the fear of God. "And if ye call on the Father, who without respect of persons judgeth according to every man's work, pass the time of your sojourning here in fear" (I Peter 1:17). God is able to heal and transform the vilest of human experience. Therefore, He has the right to judge without regard to persons. There is no favoritism in His judgement. The adulterous woman who came to Him was forgiven. There was no discussion of the reasons for her fallen lifestyle, simply the command to go and sin no more (John 8:3-11). The fallen nature of man is the problem and the reasons we use to blame someone or something else for our improper behavior only hinders us from being transformed by the power of God. If His deliverance power was limited to only moderate difficulties, then perhaps some excuses would be valid. Thank God, this is not the case. He is able to save, deliver, and heal all who call upon His name.

Today, where do we find ourselves? Look around and say, "regardless of the reasons I may lean on as justification for my sin, self-pity, depression, anger, or other improper behavior, I come to Thee, Lord, and admit I have no excuse. Heal me, Lord, and transform my life. I stand before You stripped of justification, confessing my sins, asking for Your touch. And if I have wronged others – my children, my spouse, my family, my friends or acquaintances – and been a bad example before them in my sin, forgive me. I lift their lives to You now. Into Your hands I commit them and look for Your Spirit and grace to cover them, heal them, and transform them in Your love. And today, let me live in Your Spirit. Today, let me be an example of Your grace and transforming power. Today, in the place I find myself, let my heart rejoice in You. Let me be kind to all who touch my life. And let me share Your love and light in all my words and actions."

We may never stand before multitudes in ministry. We may never do great exploits for God in the eyes of man, but let us have the grace of God to not fail in the common places of life in which He has placed us. May we have His insight to see the importance of *being* in Him for the benefit of the few He may choose to place in our lives, not ignoring the importance of our family (I Tim 3:5).

THE ONLY PATH TO BLESSING...
"THY WILL BE DONE"

Heavenly Father, we seek You for the ability to always discern Your guidance. We are easily confused and often reject Your counsel. Help us to recognize Your voice more clearly. Looking back, we can see where mistakes were made, and for those we ask and accept Your forgiveness. As we go forward, may we be more sensitive to Your instruction and quicker to obey. Transform our thinking to be submissive to the Word and the Holy Spirit. May we learn to cherish obedience regardless of the cost, that You may make us a brighter light in this world and a help to others. In Jesus' name we pray. Amen.

"OBEY, I BESEECH THEE, THE VOICE OF THE LORD...AND THY SOUL SHALL LIVE." (Jeremiah 38:20)

We are very much like Zedekiah and Israel. We have difficulty accepting the direction of the Lord and often do not understand it. Through the circumstances surrounding Israel, God was getting Zedekiah's attention, but He did not receive his obedience. In Jeremiah 38:14, Zedekiah brought the prophet Jeremiah to him to seek the counsel of God. Jeremiah told Zedekiah that he should yield to the king of Babylon and surrender. If he obeyed this word, then he and the city would be spared destruction (verse 17). This direction was certainly not easy to accept. Israel, the people who could say: "God called me; God delivered me; God established and blessed me," was now being told to surrender to the enemy or be destroyed. Go to Babylon? How could this be God's counsel? This leading of God seemed quite opposite the historic experience and the "God will bless me" attitude of Israel. When God had brought so many miraculous victories before, how could Israel surrender to the guidance Jeremiah proclaimed? Perhaps deliverance was coming from the seemingly hopeless situation and surrender would rob them of the victory. On its surface, the advice from God's prophet could be argued against sufficiently to be ignored.

Then there was Zedekiah's personal problem. He was afraid to obey Jeremiah's counsel. He feared that if he surrendered and was taken to Babylon, the Jews who had already been taken there would turn against him. (See Jeremiah 38:19.) Fear of the possible reaction of others froze Zedekiah and prevented his obedience. God always controls what happens to the obedient person. Fear of what others may or may not do is never grounds for disobedience. Zedekiah's eyes were not upon the Lord, but upon people. This will always bring confusion and lead to wrong decisions. Pride and refusal to humble oneself under the hand of God is also a factor in spiritual error. For the king to surrender was the ultimate act of humility. God had pronounced the captivity of Israel for His own reasons in judgement of their sin and disobedience. It was not a time to stand upon historic experiences and pre-conceived notions of His leading. Zedekiah did not have the insight or strength to obey, and the price he paid was catastrophic. (See Jeremiah 39:6-8.)

Johanan failed in similar fashion to obey the voice of the Lord. Being in the land after Zedekiah was taken and Jerusalem destroyed, he feared the leaders of Babylon would destroy him and the remnant of the people. (See Jeremiah chapter 41.) Johanan and the people with him had determined to enter Egypt for safety (41:17), which in the realm of natural thought could have been a good idea. Having just been invaded and destroyed, any other country would appear safer. Before going, Johanan and the people with him came to Jeremiah to enquire of the Lord. They swore to Jeremiah that whatever God told him they would do, even though they were already headed toward Egypt in their hearts (Jeremiah 42:3). God told them that if they would stay in the land, He would bless them. He addressed their fear of the king of Babylon and said to not fear him because God would deliver them out of his hand (Jeremiah, 42:10-12). In chapter 43 we see the sad rejection of God's words by Johanan and the people. They couldn't accept His advice because of the fear in their own hearts. Their eyes were upon Jerusalem's recent destruction and the apparent safety of Egypt, which God said would not be safe for them if they disobeyed.

Neither one of these examples is simple. There were many surrounding circumstances that made the guidance of the Spirit foreign to natural thought. Obedience is not always easy because of our inclination to rely upon our own reason. Having just witnessed the destruction of Jerusalem and the taking of the Jewish people into captivity, it would be difficult to accept staying in the land and expecting a blessing. The key to obedience is focus; focus upon the Lord, His word and His leading. Surrounding factors may be brought to Him in prayer, and all concerns and confusion that we may express to Him are not sin. We err when we do not take our concerns to God and then proceed away from the Spirit's leading. Zedekiah and Johanan would have prospered by continuing to reason with God about the advice received until they understood its value. Disobedience always carries with it a price that is not pleasant to pay.

Our goals and objectives must be surrendered to God. His work is different than we expect much of the time. We are inclined to look to the outcome of the "war", the condition of the "walls", and freedom from the constraints in our life as those things which are most important. God on the other hand looks upon the heart, and desires to accomplish His inner work of transformation. If we are placed on the losing side of the battle, and are surrounded by burnt and destroyed walls while we are under the direction of a "foreign king", we will yet be victorious if we learn to obey God and His inner work is accomplished in our hearts (Jeremiah 29:11).

YOU ARE OF GREAT VALUE!

Heavenly Father, Your love comforts and encourages us in the place we find ourselves. Our refuge is not in a distant land, free from the current burdens upon us, but is in Your presence in the midst of where we live. Our value in life is not measured with the scale of earthly wealth and position, but by the scale of love hung on Calvary's cross. Jesus came to earth to purchase our salvation with the price of His life and His blood. He paid the same price for each soul who will believe, for each one is of great value in Your eyes. By the example of His lowly birth and humble living, we are taught the importance of inner matters of the heart and the temporal worth of all else in this world. Help us to keep our eyes upon Your ways and values in our own lives and in the lives of others. In Jesus' name we pray. Amen.

"HAVE NOT...RESPECT OF PERSONS" (James 2:1)

In our own minds, with what do we clothe ourselves? How do we measure our value to God? Are we discouraged by our status in life? What clothing do we admire in others? Are we impressed by the outward appearance of success, position, moral correctness, or etiquette? It is our nature to be impressed with these things. It is our error to measure by them alone. Jesus seeks to help us place these things in the proper perspective. James speaks to the issue in the book of James, chapter 2, saying, "My brethren, have not the faith of our Lord Jesus Christ, the Lord of glory, with respect of persons. For if there come unto your assembly a man with a gold ring, in goodly apparel, and there come in also a poor man in vile raiment; and ye have respect to him that weareth the gay clothing, and say unto him, Sit thou here in a good place; and say to the poor, Stand thou there, or sit here under my footstool: are ye not then partial in yourselves, and are become judges of evil thoughts? Hearken, my beloved brethren, hath not God chosen the poor of this world rich in faith, and heirs of the kingdom which he hath promised to them that love him? But ye have despised the poor...if ye have respect to persons, ye commit sin, and are convinced of the law as transgressors." The world tends to blindly accept, respect, and place great value upon people in positions of authority, the rich and powerful, those with titles...God does not!

Our unregenerate nature thinks highly of those who appear to be successful. If at a later time an individual no longer holds a successful position, we tend to think less of them. We judge wrongly if we look only on the appearance or person of an individual. God sees and places value on each person equally and is not a respecter of persons (I Peter 1:17; Col. 3:25; Rom. 2:11). No one soul is more important to Him than another. While everyone is given greatly varying responsibilities in life, our value does not vary with God. God uses positions of responsibility to teach those who need such an experience.

Other seemingly lesser assignments in life are equally as important to God. Success in God's eyes is doing that which He has given with a heart attitude that is proper before Him (Col. 3:22-24). Our value in the sight of God is no greater if we are given much responsibility and it is no less if we are given little. Not everyone is given five talents (Matt. 25:14-15). Our acceptance is through faith in Jesus and His redemptive work on the cross. Our growth and reward is through obedience to Him. It is unwise to compare ourselves with another. How we perform in our individual circumstances is what is important. Even the harlot Rahab was justified in the eyes of God by her work of assisting Israel's messengers, and she was certainly not held in esteem by others (James 2:25).

Faith in Jesus is a great equalizer (James 1:9-10). The poor, the rich, the successful, the simple, the teacher, and the pupil, all must bow before the same throne of God. Hebrews 4:13 states, "...all things are naked and opened unto the eyes of him with whom we have to do." The only clothing which is accepted by the Lord is that which He gives through obedience to Him. The degree to which we are clothed with His likeness is a valid measurement, not the earthly circumstances He chooses to accomplish this goal. Through the humblest of surroundings our Lord came into this world. Through a life of rejection and ridicule he revealed the nature of God to a sinful people. Through the vilest of experiences being mocked, beaten, publicly humiliated, and crucified – He purchased our redemption.

It is wise for us to learn to see others, and ourselves, through the eyes of the Lord...of great value! We should not measure our success and worth, nor that of another, by that which is apparent, but by God's love shown us through Jesus. Responsibilities in life are given for a reason, and God teaches us to respect those in positions of authority and leadership (Romans 13:1-7). Wisdom gives us the insight to discern if any outward success is coupled with inward rightness with God, and likewise, if any apparent humility is real or superficial. Lowly surroundings do not make one humble, nor does success make one proud. The attitude of the heart alone determines these matters.

19

ARE YOU IN GOD'S HIDDEN WORKSHOP?

Oh, Lord, our God, Your ways are truly wrapped in the word mystery. To our natural understanding we can call them by no other name. We do not comprehend for we have difficulty sitting at Your feet. Stillness and patience are not things we easily adopt. We strive for understanding and yet fall short of clarity, for our reasoning leads to confusion and doubt. We too easily miss the pathway of simplicity. We too heavily lean upon our own abilities to reason. We are too easily impressed by what our senses experience and too little controlled by an understanding of Your nature and holiness. We are bombarded with enormous amounts of the world, its ways and its measurements. Protect us from such influence upon our perception of You and Your ways. Too much of what we see is mixed with unholy fire, and we are slow to discern for the dullness of our spiritual sight. Bring us to the simple and deep ways of the Spirit. Separate us unto Yourself fully, for the longing of our hearts is satisfied only by You. In Jesus' name we pray. Amen.

TWICE HIDDEN

There is a conspicuous absence of public praise and acceptance in the life of the one led by the Holy Spirit. Success in the religious world, as man measures success, is almost always missing from the life of the true saint. God has a way of hiding His own and hiding from them many of the beautiful things He does through them. Partly for our own protection, lest our ego rise to claim an ounce of glory for His working, and partly for our preparation. When there is a public presentation of the Holy Spirit through a saint, there is normally an equal balance of persecution. Perhaps equal is not quite correct. The more Jesus ministered, the more opposition mounted against Him (John 10:31). The more Paul was used of the Spirit, the more time he spent in jail or fleeing for his life (Acts 9:23). Even with the public and open moving of His Spirit, the appearance of success, as we measure it, was not there (Luke 4:28-32). It is when, through our own energies, we move to "work the works of God", that worldly success is accomplished (John 12:43). This is not the arena of ministry in which our Lord operates.

God has a way of hiding us while He prepares us for His purposes. He does not accomplish this by placing us in remote seclusion geographically, but rather in the middle of our busy world. Isaiah 49:2 states, "in the shadow of his hand hath he hid me, and made me a polished shaft." God brings His shadow over our lives in the place we find ourselves. While we are busy with daily life, God is busy polishing us to make us an effective witness for Him. Just as common cloth is used to polish fine jewelry, so the common cloth of life's experience is used by the Spirit to make us shine as a reflection of God's grace and Person. The cloth of challenge, adversity, heartbreak, sacrifice, and misunderstanding must be rubbed upon the tarnished areas of our life to bring forth the image and reflection of Jesus. When we find ourselves wondering why we are challenged on this issue or that, remember we are under His shadow for the purpose of refurbishment, rebuilding and transformation. We experience all the things common to man in our journey, but all things common are turned holy by the hand of Him who has placed us under His shadow. His hand is upon the common cloth.

And then again He hides us! Isaiah 49:2 continues, "in his quiver hath he hid me." Sharpened, polished, prepared and then placed in his quiver. Hidden again to the outside world, we find God placing His polished arrows into his quiver. God is not interested in displaying His handiwork in us as a piece of art for public appreciation. This would build our religious ego to the point of destruction. He is interested in glorifying Jesus. It is in allowing God to keep us hidden that we find protection and usefulness. If we are not content to sit in His quiver, we are not fit to be placed in His bow. Being sharpened and polished is not license for self's energies to carry forward. If we strive to be the one holding the bow, we overstep our purpose. We must ever remain in His quiver until He places the bow string upon us. Without His hand upon the bow, even the most prepared arrow will miss the mark. Hidden for preparation and hidden for service...while contrary to natural thought, it is yet the glorious place to which our Lord calls us. Will we trust Him and rest in His shadow, and find contentment in His quiver? If we will, our service will carry the sharpness and power of His anointing.

20

A PURIFIED CHARACTER

Heavenly Father, Thou Holy One, we bow before the revelation of Your greatness and glory. The more we see and understand of You, the greater our sense of gratefulness, the keener our awareness of our need for You, and the quicker our knees bend to humble ourselves before You. We are more ignorant than knowing, and by Your grace we begin to see this. In the light of Your teaching us we bow...for it is Your light which reveals our need to be humbled. It is by Your grace and nearness that we learn to say "I am the least." It is a good thing to be brought to that place where we say, "I know nothing of myself, Lord, teach Thou me." From that place today we offer our praise, and the request for our eyes to be opened anew to the wonders of Your Word. We request of You to give us a teachable spirit... not an easy task for such a willful people. Thou art able, but we must first be willing. We pray to be brought to that place of inner submission and total abandonment to You, that we might know You, for this is Your desire for us. In Jesus' name we pray. Amen.

"UNTO THE MEASURE OF THE STATURE OF THE FULNESS OF CHRIST." (Eph. 4:13)

What is the ultimate intention of God for the Christian? Is it to make him active in Christian work? Is it to loosen him in the administration of the gifts of the

Spirit? Is it to make him aggressive in evangelizing the world for Christ? The answer is, none of the above. Character...character is the primary objective of God. The great I AM is interested in bringing us to be like Jesus. It is when we rearrange God's priorities that confusion enters the Church. Without first accomplishing the primary goal of being like Christ, then all other activities of Christian practice are tarnished with human nature and satanic influence. When Christian work is undertaken without character being established by the Holy Spirit, the level of expression is beneath the intentions of God. When evangelism, gifts of the Spirit and other Christian work are placed as the central theme of emphasis, they actually hinder the accomplishment of God's goal of character. Christian work and the expression of the Holy Spirit are the outflow of spiritual character and a mature relationship with God. They are the new wine which is preserved and served from new wineskins. Character is the new wineskin that must be in place before there can be the proper containing of the new wine of the Spirit.

Through the eyes of those who have not developed Godly character in Christ, the root source of expression of Christian activity is not discernable (Hebrews 5:14). Those who stand in positions of leadership, and do not focus on the development of character as the critical foundation, actually block the way and prevent others from entering the spiritual development God intends. Looking at the book of Isaiah we can see an example of the results when the ultimate goal of God (character) is bypassed for religious activity. In Isaiah 1:10-17, we see God rejecting the previously ordained sacrifices and service of the temple. The activity was taking place and to the immature eye it appeared proper, scriptural, and ordained of God. God saw it differently. He saw that holy character was missing. God's ultimate intention was bypassed for the secondary priority of religious activity. The result was religious service which God rejected. When instruction is out of line with God's priority of developing Godly character, then the substitute priority stands in the way of entering into the way of the Spirit. This is very similar to what Jesus said of the scribes and Pharisees in Matt. 23:13: "But woe unto you, scribes and Pharisees, hypocrites! for ye shut up the kingdom of heaven against men: for ye neither go in yourselves, neither suffer ye them that are entering to go in." Those that would sincerely desire to enter into a walk in the Spirit, which leads to development of character, are easily swept up into man's priorities and thus prevented from entering the pathway of God's priority.

Through the development of character comes the true perception of the awe-inspiring holiness of God. From an enlightened platform of relationship with Jesus, through the development of His character within the believer, the work and ministry of God are anointed, holy, and glorious. From the lower level of Christian activity, which bypasses character and relationship development, we find the holy things of God sinfully handled by untransformed humanity. This was the reason God rejected the offerings in Isaiah. Isaiah 29:13 states this issue concisely: "Wherefore the Lord said, Forasmuch as this people draw near me with their mouth, and with their lips do honour me, but have removed their heart far from me, and their fear toward me is taught by the precept of men..." Teaching or ministry which preempts character is the precept of man, not the Holy Spirit. New Testament service is also subject to God's wrathful rejection (Matt. 7:21-23).

Without Holy Spirit led teaching and character development, the motives of man and the influence and confusion of Satan permeate spiritual activity. Ridiculous practices are free to enter the activity of the Church and are a disgrace to the holiness of God, slandering the precious moving of His Holy Spirit. Immature hearts become the sidetracked seekers of the next new thing, the next mysterious supposed "move of God." In ignorance, those who lack relationship and character in Christ state, "I can't understand it, and it seems strange, but it must be of God for look at all the people affected; look at the Christians who participate in it. I felt so blessed." Brothers and sisters, there is much taking place in the realm of Charismatic activity which is grossly out of order and not born of God's Holy Spirit. It is tantamount to taking the Ark of God out from the holy place and casting it into the marketplace of fallen man. Merely touching the Ark cost Uzzah his life (II Sam. 6:6-7); mishandling the holy things of the Spirit is no less of an offense to God. We need to be cautious lest we adopt the "attitude of the Athenians", who spent their time in nothing but to hear or tell some new thing (Acts 17:21). We are not to be "children, tossed to and fro, and carried about with every wind of doctrine" (Eph. 4:14).

Yielding to the secluded pathway of spiritual character development will bring the discernment and relationship with Jesus necessary to prevent deception in these last days. There is no other way to learn of Him and of His ways. As we learn to know Him, the imposter becomes very apparent. This is why the ministry of the church is to bring believers into the fullness of Christs' stature (Eph. 4:11-15). The moving of the Holy Spirit is never an embarrassment to God's majesty or holiness.

21

SALVATION IS ONLY THE BEGINNING!

Heavenly Father, praise You, for you are worthy of our praise! Touch our eyes so that blindness and ignorance may fall from our understanding. Place a fire in our hearts to seek You and serve You. Burn away the dross of complacency and lukewarm seeking. Teach us to redeem the time by wisely spending our moments in prayer, praise, and yielding to You. When the day is done, may we look back and see that we have made time for those things which are important according to Your priorities, though other things are left undone. In Jesus' name we pray. Amen.

"FOR THIS CAUSE I BOW MY KNEES UNTO THE FATHER" (Eph. 3:14)

Paul, in this scripture, expresses what he prayed for the Christians in Ephesus. His prayers are further explained in Ephesians 1:15-19. Paul begins in Eph. 1:15 saying, "after I heard of your faith in the Lord Jesus, and love unto all the saints." He was writing to Christian believers. This is important to recognize in properly grasping the fullness of the following passages. In verse 17, Paul prays that these Christians would be given the spirit of wisdom and revelation in the knowledge of the

Lord. His next request of God is that the eyes of their understanding would be enlightened. One could suppose that their understanding was just fine, as they had already expressed their belief in Jesus. They could have easily stood and proclaimed, "Oh, yes, I understand all about salvation, I know Jesus as my personal Savior." Paul knew better; he knew there was much more to understand. Salvation was not the end, but rather the beginning of enlightened understanding. Understanding salvation is the first light, which is followed by continual enlightening as we seek and yield to God. Through wisdom and revelation from the Spirit, our understanding grows as we spend time in worship, in prayer, and in the reading of God's Word.

Paul then asks that they would understand the hope of their calling. This hope must be more than salvation, because the Ephesians had believed in Jesus and His salvation and at least understood that portion of the message! Paul wanted them to know about the riches of the glory of the inheritance of the saints. He also prayed for them to know the exceeding greatness of the power of God Who had saved them. He seems here to be searching for words which could begin to describe God's power by saying the "exceeding greatness" of His power. Explaining, as he moves into chapter 2, that this great power that raised Jesus from the dead is the same power that quickened them to salvation. This mighty God who raised the battered, bruised, and dead body of Jesus to life, is the same God who has touched us and extends His power toward us as well. Indeed, it is this power that works in us! (See Ephesians 3:20.) Paul is praying they will see this truth and grow in it, not simply be satisfied to be saved and heaven bound. This Jesus, who is the head of all power and authority (above all other power or authority), is the head of the church, which is His body. We then, as a part of that spiritual body of Christ, have His life power flowing in us. It is present in us. Just as blood flows to every cell of the human body, so God's power and Spirit flow to every member of His body. To the degree that we are enlightened to understand the magnitude of this, we discover limbs and functions active in us we never knew we had. This is what Paul is praying for. Paul knew that unbelief and limited enlightenment were like a tourniquet, which would keep the life of God from fully expressing through the Christian. Paul drama- tizes his concern by saying he "bowed his knees before the Father." He was not merely praying, but was getting down on his knees before God with this very important request. Paul knew that the flow of living water and power were full to the point of the faucet, which is the Christian. He wanted the Ephesian believers to learn, grow, and yield to the flow of this life, and not be found blocking it.

As Paul speaks in the third chapter of Ephesians, he is praying for the Christians to be strengthened in the inner man; that Christ would dwell in their hearts; that they would be rooted and grounded in love; and that they would comprehend the breadth, and length, and depth and height of the Christian experience. Salvation is not to be the waiting room for heaven. There is a whole world of spiritual life, experience, and growth for the Christian. Paul is praying that we would get out of the waiting room and discover and explore the greatness of life in Christ. It is as if we were invited into the entry hall of a great mansion. Some are content to just be in the mansion and desire to go no further. The entry hall is salvation, and that is good enough for some. However, this was not good enough for Paul, nor was it what he was praying for. He desired that the Christian explore all of the rooms and glorious grounds of the entire heavenly estate...now, while in this life. For the believer who knows something of God's love and salvation, Paul prays in chapter 3:19, that the believers would "know the love of Christ, which passeth knowledge, that ye might be filled with all the fullness of God." This requires moving from the entry halls of heaven into the many rooms of the spiritual mansion which is Christ's fullness.

Ephesians 3:17 finds Paul praying that "Christ may dwell in your hearts by faith." A strange thing to say to those who had received Him into their hearts, or so it seems. However, Paul's emphasis is focused on more than initially receiving Christ. Paul is saying, "You have received Christ into your hearts through salvation. I do not want you thinking that because you are now forgiven, you may proceed through life on your own plans. On the contrary, I pray for Christ to dwell fully and completely in all of your heart until you are full of the fullness of God." To dwell means to house permanently. This is more than an occasional yielding to or seeking of God. (This does not mean a gaining and then losing of salvation, but rather a mind set that seeks to continually please God and yield to him, as compared to a casual faith in Christ while living for self-satisfaction.) Paul wanted the Ephesian believers to allow Christ to dwell permanently in their lives, and this was his prayer. He did not want them filing their salvation away as one would an insurance policy, but desired them to enter through salvation into the wonders and glories of God in the Spirit.

Through every experience in life we will find growth and greater revelation from God as we understand the purpose of life and of our salvation. We must taste of the chastening, the discipline, the trials, the testings, the love and comfort of God in order to experience the fullness of Christ. He is in all of these experiences with us. We will see the glories of heaven as we keep our eyes upon Him through each day.

22

TURNING POTENTIAL DESTRUCTION INTO BLESSING

Heavenly Father, help us to know the reality of the constant and abiding blessing of Your presence, in all of life's experiences. May this knowing be founded upon our knowledge of Your Word as quickened to our hearts by the Holy Spirit. Thank You that we dwell in You, in that place of continual blessing, a place which cannot be shaken by circumstances around us in this world. Praise You for the victory won on Calvary, paid for with Your blood, and so graciously shared with us through our faith in You and Your Word. In Jesus' name we pray. Amen.

THE PATHWAY TO THE VALLEY OF BLESSING

In II Chronicles 20:26 we read of the children of Judah assembled in the valley of Berachah, which means the valley of blessing. Here they blessed the Lord who had delivered them from the threat of destruction and blessed them with bountiful spoil from the enemy. They were so blessed that they spent three days carrying away the spoil (verse 25). They were rejoicing in the blessing of the Lord. As we have placed our trust in Jesus, we too seek His blessing. The truth is that we may dwell in His blessing continuously, if we choose His ways. The times of celebration and realized victory are special moments in our walk with the Lord, but they are not the only times of blessing. Fearful times, common times, toiling times, not-so-sure times, and times of waiting are also His times of blessing. We may not fully recognize them as such if we fail to understand the ways in which He leads us to accomplish His good work in our hearts.

The story of Jehoshaphat, King of Judah, as told in II Chronicles 20 is a good example of God's blessing being present all along the Christian journey to our valley of Berachah (blessing). Before we look specifically at this story, let us first ask ourselves what kind of person was Jehoshaphat? What were his priorities? What was it about him that would cause him to experience God's blessings? In II Chronicles 17:3-6 we see into the heart-level priorities of Jehoshaphat. "And the Lord was with Jehoshaphat, because he walked in the first ways of his father David, and sought not unto Baalim; But sought to the Lord God of his father, and walked in his commandments, and not after the doings of Israel. (Israel at this time had turned from the Lord.) Therefore the Lord stablished the kingdom in his hand...and his heart was lifted up in the ways of the Lord." Jehoshaphat determined to turn away from evil and toward the Lord. He sought God. As we read of his life, we see that his judgment was not always perfect; he made mistakes. (See II Chron.19:2.) However, God was with him because his heart was postured to seek the Lord. It is this type of inner commitment that allows God to keep us in His blessing. If we desire God's blessing, we must decide to turn away from the evil of the world

110

around us and toward the Lord and His ways. Romans 12:2 states it this way, "And be not conformed to this world: but be ye transformed by the renewing of your mind, that ye may prove what is that good and acceptable, and perfect, will of God."

Jehoshaphat's journey to the valley of blessing had an unlikely beginning. It started with the threat of destruction. II Chronicles 20:1-2 tells us that the children of Moab, the children of Ammon, and others beside them, had joined together to fight with Judah and King Jehoshaphat. Scripture tells us that this was a great multitude that had gathered against the Lord's people. Jehoshaphat feared what might happen in a battle against such a great enemy army. The possibility of death and captivity was very real based upon the natural appearance of things surrounding him. Jehoshaphat then set himself to seek the Lord, and to proclaim a fast throughout Judah. In the face of the enemy, Jehoshaphat determined to seek the Lord. (See verse 3.) When the people were gathered together, Jehoshaphat prayed. In his prayer, he acknowledged that God was a God of power who had driven out the people of the land before Israel. While he had not seen the victory in his current challenge, he rehearsed before God the previous triumphs of the Lord. He stated before God in prayer the things that God had promised His people if they were ever threatened with evil. (See verses 6-12.) Jehoshaphat had knowledge of God and His previous works. He was familiar with the Word of the Lord. When challenged with evil, he stood upon the Word and his faith in God. In verse 12 he places his life, and the life of the people of Judah, into God's hands saying, "for we have no might against this great company that cometh against us; neither know we what to do: but our eyes are upon thee." In our own challenges and seeking of God, holding up to the Lord His own Word is a powerful way to pray!

As we look at what is happening, we see that Jehoshaphat and all of Judah were already walking in the blessing of the Lord; they were involved in a very deep and real relationship with Him. They covered themselves with His Word, His previous works, His promises, and then they waited. There is no greater blessing than trusting in and waiting upon the Lord. The momentary celebration of the victory realized is no greater or lesser a blessing than the pathway of relationship that gets us there. Scripture teaches that we are already victorious through Christ! (See Romans 8:37.) Even before we realize our valley of blessing experience, our pathway is blessed by fellowship with Jesus and we are assured that the victory is certain, if we walk in His ways and are obedient to Him. We will not experience His victory with disobedient hearts.

After waiting upon the Lord, the Spirit of God came upon Jahaziel in the midst of the assembly and he prophesied, "Hearken ye, all Judah, and ye inhabitants of Jerusalem, and thou king Jehoshaphat, Thus saith the Lord unto you, Be not afraid nor dismayed by reason of this great multitude; for the battle is not yours, but

God's...Ye shall not need to fight in this battle: set yourselves, stand ye still, and see the salvation of the Lord
with you, O Judah and Jerusalem: fear not, nor be dismayed; tomorrow go out against them: for the Lord will
be with you" (verses 15-17). His salvation is with us, as
noted above, not to be given in the future, not maybe
with us if we do all things correctly, not with us sometimes,
but *is with us* (Matt. 28:20). We realize the blessings of
salvation through seeking God first, as Jehoshaphat, and
walking in obedience.

The next day, we read that as Judah began to sing
and praise God, the Lord caused the enemy army to
destroy themselves (verses 22-23). When Judah arrived,
we read, "they looked unto the multitude, and, behold,
they were dead bodies fallen to the earth, and none
escaped." God had fulfilled his word from the previous
day. They beheld the salvation of the Lord that was with
them all the time. As we keep our eyes upon Him, His
blessing is ours today and every day, as it was for
Jehoshaphat and all of Judah. Praise God, our victory is
certain in Him, as we obey.

23

RESPECTING THE HOLY SPIRIT

Holy Father, bless Your holy name! Your majesty and holiness exceed our ability to understand. We are shielded from beholding Your fullness, for our sinful frame would be consumed in the brightness of Your glory. It is Your grace that is gentle with us, as well as patient and longsuffering. At times, we treat You with too much familiarity, and by doing so we, in ignorance, show a lack of respect. Through grace we are forgiven and made comfortable in Your presence, but do not let that comfort lead to any less sanctity in our relationship with You. Thou art the Almighty! May we humble ourselves in Your presence and not forget from where we have come...even death in our sins. Thank You for life and cleansing through Jesus, in whose name we pray. Amen.

"UZZAH PUT FORTH HIS HAND TO THE ARK OF GOD" (II Sam. 6:6)

Our God is holier than we know! His glory exceeds what we are able to comprehend while yet in this body of flesh. Even Paul explained that we "see through a glass darkly," but that the day was coming when we would "know, even as we are known." (See I Cor. 13:12.) Even as God hid Himself in a cloud when communicating with the children of Israel following their exodus from Egypt, so we are somewhat shielded from the fullness of His glory even today. Those who have seen Him clearer have been moved to fall upon their faces in His presence. John, a disciple who walked with Jesus, when seeing Him in the reality of the Spirit said, in Revelations 1:17, "And when I saw him, I fell at his feet as dead." John had spent much time with Jesus and was very close to Him as a disciple. Yet, when seeing His majesty and power in the Spirit, he fell on his face. This is the supreme act of submission and humility. John, by doing so, was acknowledging the deity of Jesus. Although Jesus had called His disciples "friends," John was seeing much more than a friend: He was seeing His God.

Sometimes, as we become more conversant with the things of God – His Word, prayer, worship, and the activities that accompany the Christian faith – we can slip into behavior that is less than proper. Things can creep into our attitudes and actions that are not glorifying to the Lord. The respect and awe that should cause us to humble ourselves can be missing, or lost, if we touch the things of God with too much familiarity and too little respect and holy fear. This can lead to the flavor and leaven of the world polluting our testimony and lifestyle. If we are careless with the things that are holy, we stand on dangerous ground in the Spirit, though we are under grace. Deception, error, and sin await us if we step into the wrong heart attitude concerning God and the spiritual things of ministry. To touch the things of God today, in Christian service and witness, is to touch the same holiness kept in the Ark of God in Old Testament times. He is the same God yesterday, today and forever. While we are under grace and not under the law, still we are wise to guard our hearts against any attitude that would tarnish the ways of the Spirit or cast a worldly or lower nature hue upon the things of God.

Uzzah fell into this trap of being too familiar with the holiness of God. During the wars of Israel, the ark of God had found itself in the house of Abinadab. David, once secure upon the throne as king, desired to bring the ark to Jerusalem. This became a great event. David took with him thirty thousand men, and with all the people went to bring the ark from the house of Abinadab. The ark was placed upon a wooden cart that was pulled by oxen. The two sons of Abinadab, Ahio and Uzzah, led the cart. God had given very specific instructions concerning the ark: who could carry it and how it was to be handled. The ark was to be carried by the Levites on their shoulders using the staves God had instructed to be made for that purpose. (See Numbers, 4:5-6.) It was not to be carried on a cart, which was how the Philistines returned the ark to Israel (I Sam. 6:7). Further, the ark was not to be touched by even the Levites, under the penalty of death (Numbers 4:15). Perhaps we would judge this a small detail, but God demands that we respect His instructions and thus show respect for Him. As they traveled, the movement of the oxen shook the cart as they approached Nachon's threshing floor. Uzzah put forth his hand to prevent the ark from falling. This angered God, for in treating the ark with unholy familiarity, Uzzah had crossed the line and disobeyed the Word of God. This transgression cost Uzzah his life (II Sam. 6:7).

Perhaps Uzzah became too comfortable with the ark while it remained in his father's house. The holiness of the ark had not changed, nor had God's instructed attitude toward it, but Uzzah's attitude was disrespectful. Handling the ark in the same fashion that the nonbelieving Philistines had done was the first mistake (the cart pulled by oxen). The ways of the world had affected the way Israel was approaching God. Later, in I Chronicles 15, we read of David returning to properly bring the ark to Jerusalem. In verse two he says, "none ought to carry the ark of God but the Levites." In verse 13 David acknowledges the prior error saying, "For because ye did it not at the first, the Lord our God made a breach upon us, for that we sought him not after the due order."

This story demonstrates the dangers of allowing an attitude to develop which is too casual in its approach to God. Such an attitude demeans the holiness of the Lord and grieves the Holy Spirit. It finds as its source the darkness of the world around us and the hateful influence of Satan: the one who shows no respect for God and His authority. A good measure of holy fear is healthy in our handling the things of God. Without it we could easily be found to place the glories of the Spirit on a wooden cart behind oxen; a place God never intended them to be. The ark was to be carried by wooden staves placed through four golden rings attached to the ark. We too must learn to handle the things of the Spirit with the "wood" of humility and the "gold" of holiness. Any influence from the flesh or the world must be rejected, for the things of the Spirit are not to be handled with such things.

24

LIFE'S RESTRICTIONS...
HOW THEY BLESS US

Heavenly Father, Shepherd of our souls, forgive us for our impetuous ways and impatient hearts. Forgive us for our lack of faith, which we have often displayed through our questioning of the way You have placed before us. We acknowledge You in all things. In the common moments, yes in every moment, we acknowledge You as the Lord of that moment. You know precisely the purpose of every detail of our lives. Everything around us, we place upon the altar and give it unto You. We do not wish to escape it, but rather to learn from it the gem of light You wish to give. Though we may struggle to understand, we trust You, and know that the precious Holy Spirit will help us to yield, for our desire is to fulfill Your will. Thank You for the Teacher, who is able to enlighten our hearts. In Jesus' name we pray. Amen.

"WHATSOEVER TOUCHETH THE ALTAR SHALL BE HOLY." (Exodus 29:37)

The Lord takes the things most common, and transforms them into things most holy. Common sheep and livestock, dwelling in the fields and fences of God's people, became holy offerings unto God when placed upon the altar of sacrifice. The altar sanctified the gift (Matt.23:19). The gift of itself was not a holy thing. The one thing that separated one sheep from another, to make it holy, was not the beauty of the pasture in which it dwelt, nor the cleanliness of its wool, but the altar upon which it was offered. The altar of sacrifice made the offering holy and acceptable to God. The correct altar made the common into something holy.

There is an altar of sacrifice today that serves the same purpose. It is in the temple of the Lord, just as the altar of old. However, the temple has changed. The temple of God is now the heart of the believer. Scripture teaches us that we are the temple of the Holy Spirit (I Cor. 6:19). Therefore, all that we offer upon the altar of our hearts becomes holy unto the Lord. Further, all that touches our life, which we offer unto the Lord, becomes something that God uses to further His purposes in our growth and walk with Him. In fact, there is nothing that touches our life that does not become an instrument in the Master's loving hand, to be used for our edification and benefit, when offered to Him in an attitude of willing sacrifice. It is when we struggle against the instruments He chooses that we create more pain for ourselves and hinder His loving work. As we willingly place all things upon the altar of total yielding, we discover more quickly the lesson to be learned.

God uses every circumstance in our lives to discipline our souls and enlighten our minds to understand His ways. The pressures, restrictions, responsibilities, and adversities are necessary for our growth. The Lord takes the valleys of our lives when it is difficult to continue, the mountainous terrain that seems impassable, the crooked paths where we cannot see, and the rough places that seem too challenging, and through them reveals His glory to us (Isaiah 40:1-5). It is when we question them that we delay the process of spiritual development. Every common thing that touches our lives, when offered upon the altar of our heart, is swiftly transformed into an instrument of light that opens our eyes to better understand the Lord. God is in the limits and restrictions of our lives, and it is when we acknowledge Him in all things that we find enlightenment. It is faith that enables us to acknowledge Him in everything that touches our lives. It requires this faith to please Him. This inner action is quite different from the impostor of religious activity.

In John 10, Jesus speaks of being the door to the sheep. He speaks also of others trying to climb in without coming through the Door. The picture we see is one of an enclosed area with a door and fences or walls. This must be the case, for if He were speaking only of open pastures, there would be no door, nor anything to climb over. The picture portrays some restrictions placed upon His sheep. They were behind the door, and inside the fences. It is inside the restrictions of life that we learn to hear His voice and understand His ways. It is the impostor that romps, undisciplined, in the pastures outside the sheepfold of the Spirit. It was the impostor that attempted to climb into the sheepfold, bypassing the Door, to get at the sheep (John 10:1). When Jesus did lead the sheep out of the fold, they had become familiar with His voice. Because of this, they could stay close to Him in the freedom of the open pastures (John 10:3-5). The discipline learned inside the limits of the fold prepares the soul for a spiritual walk when the limits are relaxed or removed.

If we understand the way of the Spirit, we then know that the perceived limitations and the responsibilities of life are the fences of God's love that protect us until we have become so yielded to Him that, even without fences, we would walk only in the steps of our Shepherd and not dare go astray. Those who listen to the impostor, jump the fences, into seemingly glorious freedom, premature to learning the deeper disciplines of the Lord. The pastures are full of religious impostors that cannot lead the sheep to the deeper truths of the Spirit. It is the impostor that attempts to tell us the fences and disciplines of God's sheepfold are not spiritual and should be ignored. The truth is, that the true freedom and revelation of the Holy Spirit come to us as we accept the apparent limitations and restrictions. It is by yielding to them, not avoiding or resisting them, that we find our eyes opened and our hearts filled with His presence. It is when we place the fences around our lives upon the altar of our heart that our spirit is freed from selfishness and sin. Leaping with the impostor through the fields of religious works is not the way of the Spirit. We must learn the disciplines of God's fences to grow in the Spirit. They are for our protection and blessing.

Faith and trust in God allow us to live day by day, knowing that our steps are ordered by the Lord. We do not need to question the path. We do not need to figure out a better way. We can trust in His wisdom and yield to the order of the day, for it is His order. We can rest in the fold and not press against the fences, for our Shepherd has placed us here for our benefit. We must learn to hear His voice and distinguish it from the imposter, before we dare venture into the open pastures. There are dangers in the outer pastures for which He is preparing us, as we are willing to rest in the fold of His choosing. It is inside the fold that our will is sacrificed and His is learned. When His will has become ours, we will no longer see any fences, nor valleys, nor mountains, nor rough or crooked places, but only our Shepherd.

GOD HEARS YOUR PRAYERS

Heavenly Father, forgive us for our misunderstanding as it relates to the wonders of Your grace. We rejoice to know that through faith we are saved and justified in Your eyes, not by our own works. Keep us from the bondage of thinking that our own efforts improve us in Your sight. Let us forever stay focused upon the glorious sacrifice of Jesus and the greatness and perfection of His name. We are awed by the power of the name in which we pray: the name of Jesus. Amen.

"AND HIS NAME, THROUGH FAITH IN HIS NAME."

(Acts 3:16)

What can I add to my prayers to make them more effective? In the Old Testament of the Bible, man was required to bring sacrifices and offerings to God. Some of these were sin offerings, while others were to demonstrate thankfulness. Are there offerings or sacrifices that I can bring today to improve my chances of getting an answer to my prayers? This question has a strange ring...and it should. Such thinking rings of works rather than faith. "What can I do?" " What can I add?" "What can I bring to get more of God's attention and response?" These are questions that lead toward our own effort in attempting to become better in God's eyes. The initial question of, "how can my prayers become more effective," is a good question. Where we take our search for the answer is a possible area of concern. We may choose from many paths in our walk with God. It is possible to take a wrong turn. Sound teaching in the things of the Spirit will help us to make the correct choice. These are not necessarily paths in the physical world, but in the world of thought and spirit. Mind sets develop which, if we are not careful, can sidetrack us in the realm of the spirit.

Thinking which takes us away from the simplicity and power of faith is destructive. It is grieving to the work of the Holy Spirit and brings bondage to our souls. Paul watched with great concern as the Galatians were swept up with a similar mind set. They were attempting to add works to the foundation of faith in Jesus. They were "thinking" that by doing certain things they would become more acceptable to God. They yielded to the wrong concept: adding the works of the law to their faith in Jesus. Paul called this thinking a perversion of the Gospel of Christ. (See Gal. 1:7.) Any such thinking is opposite to the teachings of Jesus, the receiving of salvation, and the indwelling of the Holy Spirit. Paul asked the Galatians in chapter 3, verses 2-3, "This only would I learn of you, received ye the Spirit by the works of the law, or by the hearing of faith? Are ye so foolish? Having begun in the Spirit, are ye now made perfect by the flesh?" He previously stated to them, "even we have believed in Jesus Christ, that we might be justified by the faith of Christ, and not by the works of the law: for by the works of the law shall no flesh be justified" (Gal. 2:16). "For in Jesus Christ neither circumcision availeth any thing, nor uncircumcision; but faith which worketh by love" (Gal. 5:6). Thinking which makes me perform, in order to receive favor from God, takes me out of God's grace and places me under a form of religious law. This is a realm in which faith is inoperative. In Gal 5:4, Paul says that if I place the burden of righteousness upon myself, and think to accomplish it by my works, then I have fallen from grace.

The same principle holds true concerning my prayers. I cannot add anything to them to make them more effective. If I bind myself with a vow to display to God how serious I am about my request, it does not add effectiveness to my prayers. If I pledge to do acts of good-ness continually, or to not do certain things that displease Him ever again, even then I add nothing to the power of my prayers. The secret of effective praying is faith and obedience: faith in His name and faith in His sacrifice. When Jesus was asked, " what must man do to work the works of God," He said, "This is the work of God, that ye believe on him whom he hath sent" (John 6:28-29). Jesus tells us to pray in His name. "And *whatsoever* ye shall ask in my name, that will I do, that the Father may be glorified in the Son." (See John 14:13; 15:16.) A foundational truth to effective prayer is not only faith, but obedience to God. John 15:7 says, "If ye abide in me, and my words abide in you, ye shall ask what ye will, and it shall be done unto you." The "if" is up to us. If we yield our hearts to obey, then our prayers hold great power. Without this foundation, we cannot expect God to answer our prayers. We may be praying for many things and He will bring us back to the point of obedience, which point may not be anywhere near the subject matter of our *unyielded* prayers.

When we come to God in prayer, we need to come holding up the name of Jesus. There is no more powerful way to pray. When we come in His name, we come with full access to God. God the Father gives us His full attention when we come in His Son's name. How much faith we place in His name is the key. Good works do not add any power to the name of Jesus. Acts of sacrifice do not make His name more effective with the Father. We cannot add to His name, nor to His sacrifice. Jesus' shed blood is the complete and perfect sacrifice which opens fully heaven's doors, and God's heart, to the believer. It is a mistake to think we need to add acts of duty or sacrifice to each prayer to get them through to God. We would soon be needing a log book to keep track of everything we promised God. Such a stance is folly and not of faith. If we think to add our works to what Jesus has already accomplished, then, in our own hearts, we cheapen His sacrifice and weaken His name. Ponder this for a moment: what could we add to the holy blood of Christ to make us more acceptable to God? Shall we add a week of fasting? Shall we add a large sum of money to tithe? Shall we pledge to do good deeds daily for the rest of our life? Clearly, the answer to each of these is, nothing can add to the precious work of Jesus in offering Himself as the sacrifice for our sins. And, as we think about His name, what could we possibly add to make the name of Jesus more acceptable to the Father. Foolish thinking, isn't it!

Therefore, when we pray, let us take hold of His name wholeheartedly! Let us place our utmost confidence in the fact that when we come to prayer in His name, we are heard! He has promised! It is holy fact that God will listen, regardless of our flaws and lack of perfection. To place faith in anything other than His name is sin. How dare we think that even the best of our own efforts could ever add anything to His wonderful and glorious name. When the lame man was healed in Acts 3, Peter explained, "Ye men of Israel, why marvel ye at this? or why look ye so earnestly on us, as though by our own power or holiness we had made this man to walk?…His name, through faith in His name hath made this man strong whom ye see and know: yea, the faith which is by Him hath given him this perfect soundness in the presence of you all" (Acts 3:12 & 16). Praise God! He has given us the ultimate and complete key to effective prayer: the blood of Jesus to cleanse us and make us accepted of God, and the Name of Jesus to use when we approach His holy throne. Faith and obedience are the only ingredients to be added. (See Hebrews 11:6.)

THE EXCELLENT WAY OF LOVE

Heavenly Father, with each passing day You impress us yet more with Your love and concern for our souls. You look past our misunderstandings and encourage us with Your wisdom and instruction. You are a gentle husbandman who works carefully in the garden of our hearts. You prune the dead and non-productive branches to encourage a more fruitful expression. The motive of Your work is love, and for this we thank You and praise You. This love was embodied in the coming of Jesus to this earth. This was the great love of God, that Jesus should lay down His life for sinful man. Thank You Lord. We are grateful for our salvation. In Jesus' name we pray. Amen.

"A MORE EXCELLENT WAY" (I Cor. 12:31)

Love! God's love for man moved Him to send Jesus as the sacrifice for sin. As certain shepherds stood in the field the night Jesus was born, they were greeted by an angel. The message from this angel was, "behold, I bring you good tidings of great joy, which shall be to all people. For unto you is born this day in the city of David a Savior, which is Christ the Lord" (Luke 2:10). This was a tremendous message of "great joy." How excited this angel must have been to be able to announce Jesus' birth. Other heavenly beings were standing by listening to the announcement. Once the angel had made his proclamation, they could no longer be silent. The news was too exciting! They had to join in, as we read in verse 13, "And suddenly there was with the angel a multitude of the heavenly host praising God, and saying, Glory to God in the highest, and on earth peace, good will toward men."

How stunned these shepherds must have been. They were taken up in the moment, as a multitude of spiritual heavenly beings were proclaiming glory to God and good will toward men. They heard first hand the wondrous news of the Saviors' birth, as they were lifted from the pastures in which they stood into the presence of God's glory. Heaven was excited on this day when Jesus was born. The announcement reflected their great joy and enthusiasm over what had occurred. This was a very big occasion. The Lamb of God had been born. Not merely another sacrifice upon the altar under the law, but the final sacrifice for man's sin. Jesus was the one who would pay the final and complete price to redeem man to God. All of the sacrifices under the law could not add up to pay for this purchase. They fell short in the books of heaven. The blood of bulls and goats was not valuable enough to pay for the soul of man. It would take the blood of the Lamb of God, Jesus! (Hebrews 9:13-14; 25-28;10:1.)

The law did well in defining sin. As Paul said, "I had not known sin, but by the law: for I had not known lust, except the law had said, thou shalt not covet" (Romans 7:7; also see Romans 7:13). The problem lay in the fact that the law was spiritual, and man was carnal. Man could not attain unto the righteousness required by the law. Man kept falling short. Thus, man kept offering sacrifices for his sin, over and over again. The problem of sin in man was an inner problem, deep within the heart. The law could not reach this area with any transforming power. This problem could only be fixed by an indwelling of holiness. The Spirit of God would have to enter the heart of man to fix the problem from the inside out. The law only addressed the outer issue of showing sin to be sin, and of offering the shedding of blood to cover the act of sin. It did not strike at the root of sin. It did not transform the sinner into a new creature.

God knew of the problem. His love desired man to be free from sin on the inside. So we read of God's gift to man in Romans 8:3-4. "For what the law could not do, in that it was weak through the flesh, God sending his own Son in the likeness of sinful flesh, and for sin, condemned sin in the flesh: that the righteousness of the law might be fulfilled in us, who walk not after the flesh, but after the Spirit." God said, "I will fix the problem. I will cleanse man from all of his sin with the blood of my Son. I will make him holy in My sight, so that I might indwell him with My Spirit. I will give man the power to overcome from within."

The "New Covenant" in Jesus' blood was designed to write God's laws within our heart. This was the inward solution to the problem. From within our own hearts we were to see, know, and be empowered, to live up to the righteousness of God. This was made possible because of His presence within us, not because of our own power or goodness. Hebrews 8:10 reads, "For this is the covenant that I will make with the house of Israel after those days, saith the Lord; I will put my laws into their mind, and write them in their hearts: and I will be to them a God, and they shall be to me a people." It is no wonder the angel and the hosts of heaven were excited to announce the birth of Jesus. A glorious mystery was unfolding before their eyes.

Goodwill toward man was the message from the hosts of heaven; God's love reaching out to us while we were yet in sin. This is the motive of all that God desires to accomplish in our hearts and lives as Christians. God loves us when He chastens us, and seeks to bring us into a place of greater blessing and righteousness. God loves us when we are struggling, and does not condemn us for our yet untransformed imperfections. God loves us when we fall and seek recovery. God wants those who reject Him to receive His love, if only they will ask. God cares deeply for all mankind, for it was to all men that the good tidings were heralded.

Paul, in chapter 13 of I Corinthians, speaks of the more excellent way of love, or charity. Not to oversimplify or take away from the gems in this chapter, however it could be written in one word. Jesus! For all of the attributes of love, as described in this chapter, are found in the life and expression of Jesus while He was on the earth. He had all power, knowledge and wisdom, yet came with over-flowing compassion and concern to touch the battered and suffering lives of many. He forgave the adulteress that others sought to condemn. He was the fullness of the good tidings and great joy over which all of heaven rejoiced. He is the more excellent way! May His Spirit and love find more expression through us, and may our hearts and minds be kept in the way that is truly more excellent – the way of God's love.

Also Available From
Spirit of Truth Publications

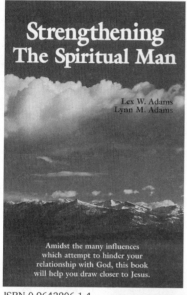

ISBN 0-9643206-1-4

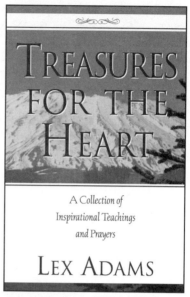

ISBN 0-9643206-0-6

CD and Tape Copies Available
(songs)

Inquire at your local Christian Bookstore

or you may order from

Spirit of Truth Publications
P.O. Box 2979
Minden, NV 89423